LOUIS HELLMAN
ARCHITECTURE
BEGINNERS

Writers and Readers

ARCHITECTURE
FOR BEGINNERS

Louis Hellman

Writers & Readers

Acknowledgments

Our thanks to Glenn Thompson, Linda Briggs, John Maddison, Anne Tauté, Philip Boys and Andrew Popkiewicz for their contributions to this book.

WRITERS AND READERS PUBLISHING, INC.

P.O. Box 461, Village Station
New York, NY 10014

Writers and Readers Limited
9 Cynthia Street
London N1 9JF
England
•

A Writers and Readers Documentary Comic Book
Copyright © 1984
ISBN # 0-86316-0-417 Trade
3 4 5 6 7 8 9 0

Manufactured in the United States of America

Beginners Documentary Comic Books are published by Writers and Readers Publishing, Inc. Its trademark, consisting of the words "For Beginners, Writers and Readers Documentary Comic Books" and the Writers and Readers logo, is registered in the U. S. Patent and Trademark Office and in other countries.

Writers and Readers—
publishing FOR BEGINNERS™ books
continuously since 1975:

1975: Cuba • 1976: Marx • 1977: Lenin • 1978: Nuclear Power • 1979: Einstein • Freud • 1980: Mao • Trotsky • 1981: Capitalism • 1982: Darwin • Economists • French Revolution • Marx's Kapital • French Revolution • Food • Ecology • 1983: DNA • Ireland • 1984: London • Peace • Medicine • Orwell • Reagan • Nicaragua • Black History • 1985: Marx Diary • 1986: Zen • Psychiatry • Reich • Socialism • Computers • Brecht • Elvis • 1988: Architecture • Sex • JFK • Virginia Woolf • 1990: Nietzsche • Plato • Malcolm X • Judaism • 1991: WW II • Erotica • African History I1992:Philosophy • Rainforests • Malcolm X • Miles Davis • Islam • Pan Africanism • 1993: Psychiatry • Black Women • Arabs & Israel • Freud • 1994: Babies • Foucault • Heidegger • Hemingway • Classical Music • 1995: Jazz • Jewish Holocaust • Health Care • Domestic Violence • Sartre • United Nations • Black Holocaust • Black Panthers • Martial Arts • History of Clowns • 1996: Opera • Biology • Saussure • UNICEF • Kierkegaard • Addiction & Recovery • I Ching • Buddha • Derrida • Chomsky • McLuhan • Jung • 1997: Lacan • Shakespeare • Structuralism

---

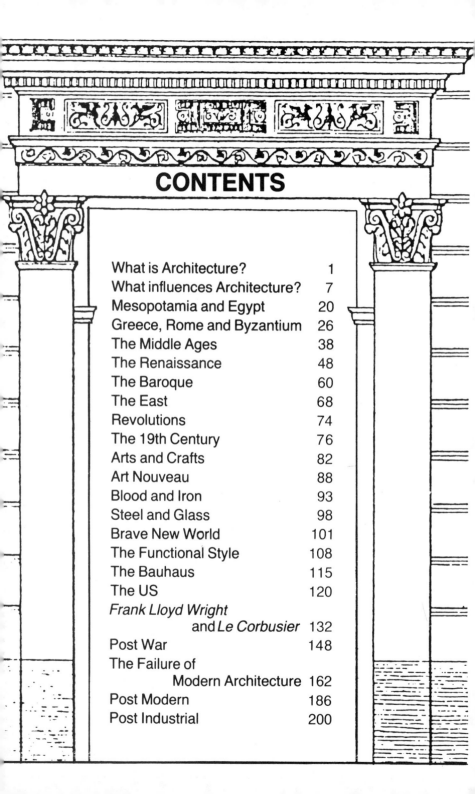

CONTENTS

WHAT IS ARCHITECTURE?

Let's start by defining the word ... What can we learn from the famous (and infamous) experts in the field?

architecture 1. The art and science of designing and building structures...

HELP! THIS ISN'T GETTING US ANYWHERE. THERE SEEM TO BE AS MANY DEFINITIONS AS THERE ARE PEOPLE!

RIGHT! ALL WE CAN SAY IS THAT ARCHITECTURE IS ABOUT PEOPLE!

ISN'T THAT PRETTY OBVIOUS?

YES, BUT OFTEN WE LOSE SIGHT OF THE OBVIOUS

3

Difficult one ... All buildings have an architect (architect means literally "chief builder") whether a professional or do-it-yourselfer — who conceives the form of the building beforehand.

We could say that *architecture* is the concept or idea which uses ... the medium of *building*, the process or technique, to communicate.

Isn't architecture an *art* then?

Yes, but not an isolated, museum art ... It's an art that affects *everybody* ... Everybody experiences architecture, like it or not.

You don't *have* to look at modern paintings or listen to modern music if you don't want to, but if a new building goes up in your neighbourhood ... you can't avoid seeing it.

Well, not just "see" it ... Architecture communicates via a whole range of stimuli...

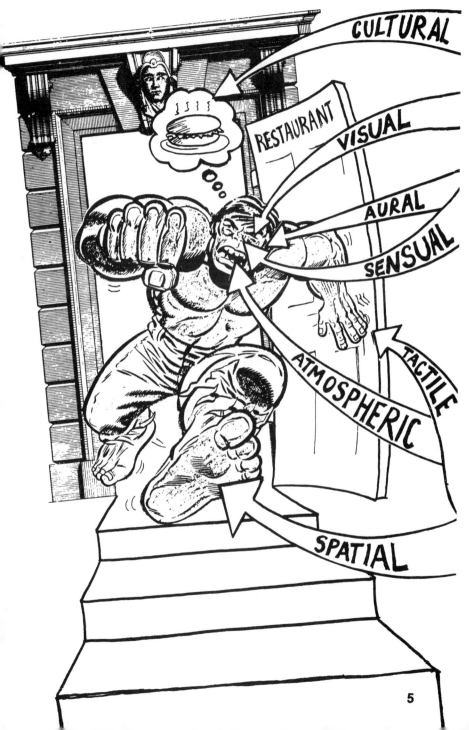

5

So architecture, being an art, communicates...and, like all art, it can be disturbing, inspiring, alienating, transcending...depending on the goals, conscious or unconscious, of the people who instigate and design it.

Architecture is subject to wide social, political or cultural influences. It reflects society and communicates the values of that society.

Yes, folks, architecture is, as the guide books say, Living History...unwritten records which are as revealing as any document.

For convenience, we can distinguish five influences on architecture: needs, society, technology, culture and climate.

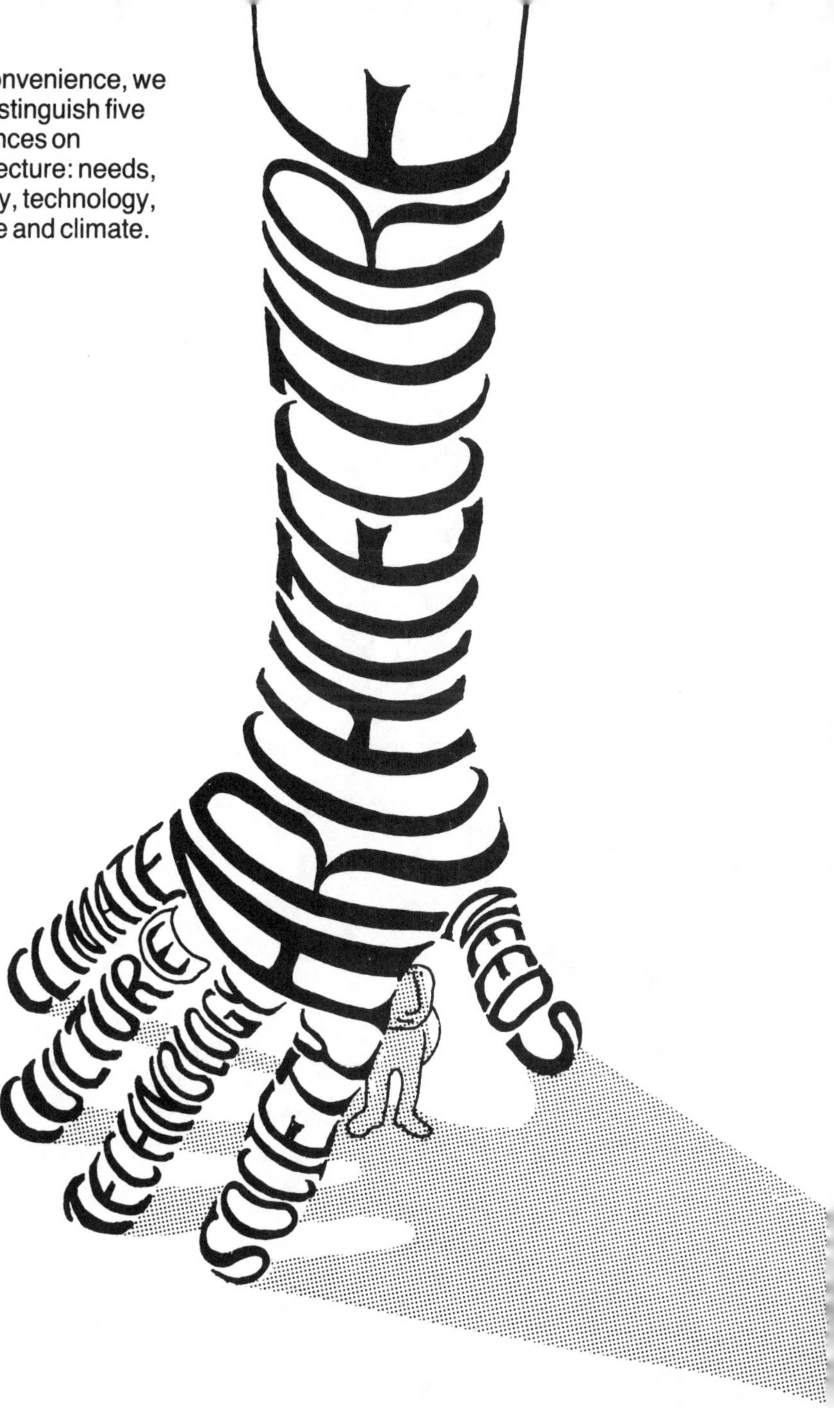

ARCHITECTURE

NEEDS

SOCIETY

TECHNOLOGY

CULTURE

CLIMATE

These influences can be illustrated by starting at the very beginning, long before professional architects existed... back in the Stone Age...

NEEDS   Why do people need buildings?

When the Great Architect in the sky designed people she made them similar to animals...

To help them survive all kinds of environments

animals are equipped with fur or claws...

Some even carry a shelter around with them...

But once people lost their hair and teeth they could no longer survive alone in environments...

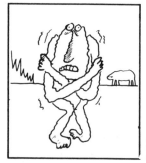

Where it is very cold...

or very hot...

YUM !

or very dangerous.

Young animals need shelter (nests, dens, holes) but very quickly grow up and leave...

They know how to cope with the world by instinct...

For human children the process takes much longer...

Humans are born with a few basic desires... but most behaviour has to be learned from the family... or the group of families or tribe.

Human children have to be protected for more than 10 years, so the family needs to stay together for a long time... usually for life.

In the Stone Age, when people gathered, fished and hunted food over great areas, they used natural shelters, particularly caves, which could be protected and defended.

TECHNOLOGY   How people build buildings

The Great Architect gave people two
important advantages over the animals...
large brains and a pair of hands.

In combination these
compensated for other
deficiencies by developing
technology...

Making tools from sticks, leather,
flakes of stone, flint or bone.

Making clothes for
survival in the heat...

or the cold...

...and weapons for
defence and hunting.

With tools people could make simple shelters where no natural ones
existed.

Building technology was conditioned by the environment. Dwellings were
built of timber in forest areas, stone in hilly places, skins on grassy plains
and deserts, and ice in the arctic.

In the New Stone Age, people discovered that by planting seeds, food could be grown near the home. They didn't have to go out looking for it.

By means of agriculture, people became food-producing. Cows and sheep could be tamed and kept as walking larders and wardrobes. Each social group was self-sufficient.

Now people needed to live where there was good land for farming. Tools and technology enabled them to build permanent dwellings which at first resembled the old cave homes.

CULTURE Buildings also have meaning

The Great Architect divided the human brain into two parts, one dealing with logic and reason, the other with intuition and imagination. People developed tools for communication... language.

Language stimulates thoughts and ideas... and the pooling of experience. Not just about the "real" world... but also about spiritual matters... magic, god, life after death.

People created a spiritual environment based on ideology, rituals related to religion, magic or tribal loyalty.

Rituals employed signs and symbols invested with special meaning ... dance, music, masks, body decoration.

Specialised buildings evolved where ceremonies and rituals were performed.

In contrast to dwellings, religious monuments were often large and built to last out of permanent materials.

Burial places were marked, perhaps first by a simple reed shrine...

The burial place became a mound... the shrine a wooden sacrificial temple...

Eventually the mound and temple evolved into the stone-built MONUMENT.

Stonehenge in England is one of the largest. Formed of three rings of stone, it might have been a place for sacrificial rites, a clock or a calendar. It is not known exactly how such a complex and sophisticated structure was erected, but there are plenty of theories...

CLIMATE How shelter deals with the elements

Just to make things more interesting the Great Architect designed in a whole lot of exciting weather around Earth.

People's dwellings had to serve as filters to modify the climate...

Letting light, air, sun *in.*

Keeping rain and noise *out.*

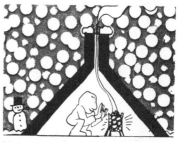

Keeping the cold out, keeping heat *in.*

In other words, people created comfortable artificial environments within the potentially hostile natural environment.

There are three basic types of climate in the world: hot and dry, cold and wet, or hot and humid. Buildings have been adapted to cope with these by using local materials and technology.

In hot dry areas thick walls keep out the heat by day, light colours reflect the sun's rays and small windows minimise glare.

At night the heat retained in the thick walls is given off to compensate for the cooler temperature.

Where it is cold and wet thick dark walls of brick or wood both keep out the cold *and* store heat. As the sky is less bright, larger windows are needed.

Steeply pitched roofs throw off rain and snow while shutters protect openings from wind. Buildings grouped in tight clusters afford outside shelter.

In tropical regions where it is hot and humid walls become open screens to let air pass through but keep out the heat. Verandahs and roof overhangs provide shaded outdoor "rooms".

In the rainy season shallow-pitched, overhanging roofs throw off the rain. Buildings may be up on stilts to guard against floods and keep out insects and reptiles.

SOCIETY Architecture with a big A

With the discovery of metals the Stone Age village life of tribal cooperation was doomed. Metals revolutionised technology and fundamentally changed society.

Tools and weapons were now more efficient. They could be moulded to any shape, re-sharpened or repaired.

The change from rough ore to hard metal seemed like magic and those who knew the secret like magicians.

Metallurgists became itinerant, selling their skills to the highest bidder and forming a separate clan or superior class.

The tribe now had to produce a surplus to support the specialist metal worker who no longer needed to farm for a livelihood.

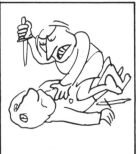

Instead of sharing, people accumulated personal property...

Leading to private wealth, jealousy and war...

The conquering tribe made the defeated into slaves.

With the rise of class, property, wealth and power came **Monumental Architecture.**

The specialist class took over religious rites, looked after the affairs of the gods and administered the surplus produce ...

It evolved into a secret society and soon the distinction between priest, god and king became blurred.

The priests ruled through a secondary class of specialist craftsmen and administrators also based in the temple.

They inhabited a temple built high on an artificial hill from where they administered the gods' affairs and stored the surplus.

The temple was the largest building, raised up above the mass of ordinary dwellings, an expression of the power of the ruling elite.

We have analysed five major influences at work on architecture. But these should not be taken too literally or deterministically. Architecture, like all art, is a synthesis of thought and feeling, external pressures and individual creativity. Analysis, like descriptions or photographs, is only a *guide* to the reality.

At any one time, one influence may predominate over another in a seemingly "irrational" way. People do not build (or do much else) according to pure logic.

For example, cultural aspects may override climatic ones. Some tribes in hot climates believe shadows contain evil spirits so they build to avoid shade.

Or social and political influences may dominate the cultural. The buildings Imperial Rome erected in conquered lands deliberately ignored local traditions and climate to suppress the people and demonstrate the might of the Empire.

The history of architecture is usually presented as the history of monuments...large, expensive, built to last... categorised according to historical styles. Monumental Architecture expresses the dominance and influence of ruling elites at any one time... "Powerful", "awe-inspiring", "impressive" are adjectives commonly used to describe it.

Challenging the historian's presentation of buildings as art objects isolated from society, this book is not so much about the History of Architecture, as the Architecture of History.

19

CIVILISATION 5000 BC – 4 AD

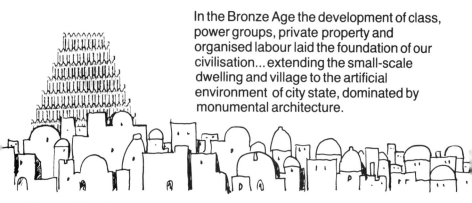

In the Bronze Age the development of class, power groups, private property and organised labour laid the foundation of our civilisation... extending the small-scale dwelling and village to the artificial environment of city state, dominated by monumental architecture.

Bronze Age civilisations grew up in three areas: in the Middle East, India and China, in valleys of fertile rivers ideal for agriculture and farming. Flood waters were controlled by means of irrigation and a large food surplus produced to buy imported materials and support capital projects.

Large scale projects involving mass slave labour required organisation and planning...

In order to keep a check on materials, the priests developed methods of counting and writing.

To predict the best time for sowing crops, they worked out a sundial calendar and sought to predict the future through astrology.

Measurement in building was originally the "cubit" or arm-length. But for large-scale projects this was obviously inadequate.

The standard measure was devised using a wooden or metal rod marked off into units.

EVER GET THE FEELING YOU'RE BEING WATCHED?

In the Middle East the first civilisations developed around the river deltas in Chaldaea (3000 – 1250 BC), where the walled cities of Ur and Babylon were raised up on platforms clear of floods.

Towering above the city of Ur was this "ziggurat" or "holy mountain", which could be seen for miles in the flat countryside. At the summit was the temple (so the priests could be near the gods), with granaries, stores and craft workshops lower down.

Through laying square floor tiles and counting stacks of bricks, methods of calculating area and volume evolved.

The architects of the temples were, of course, the priests, who put it about that they received the plans direct from the gods while they slept. (Some architects today still seem to believe this.)

21

In Mesopotamia there were few trees and little usable stone so these had to be imported at considerable expense. There was, however, plenty of one material... mud for making a substitute for stone, namely sun-dried bricks. At first shaped by hand, they were later mass-produced in moulds.

Bronze age technology improved the shaping and jointing of building materials. Monumental buildings exploited the wall. Constructed of bricks glazed on the outside in bright colours, walls were pierced by small openings and formed inner courtyards protected from the sun.

Civilisation also brought with it organised war between states, and imperialism. Defeated cities were incorporated into the victorious state. Babylon was taken over by the Assyrians (1250 – 606 BC), a cruel and militaristic people from the north who ruled from ostentatious palace fortresses.

ANCIENT EGYPT (3500 BC – 324 BC)

Egypt provided another feature of civilisation... the totalitarian dictator. The various clans and villages were subjugated under one ruler, the Pharaoh, who was god, king and high priest in one. He owned all the land and its surplus product.

WHO SAYS YOU CAN'T TAKE IT WITH YOU?

The symbol of the Pharaoh's power was the pyramid tomb. Obsessed with the preservation of the body after death, the Pharoahs used the food surplus to finance vast pyramids which contained their embalmed bodies and worldly riches for the after life.

A royal household, priesthood and civil service administered the state under a system of nepotism — the children of the pharaohs and bureaucrats were exempt from manual work and succeeded to their parents' position automatically.

The civil service improved mathematics and writing (on clay and papyrus). These skills they kept to themselves and so maintained control. In this way planning and ideas became separate from doing and making.

The pyramids are famous as the timeless symbols of the static nature of Egyptian society which hardly changed for over 4000 years. But the Egyptians' most important contribution to architecture was the COLONNADE, the COLUMN and LINTEL arrangement repeated in rows, usually within temples.

The columns were decorated with tops (CAPITALS) in the form of lotus buds, palms or papyrus flowers — symbols of the abundance and fertility of the Nile.

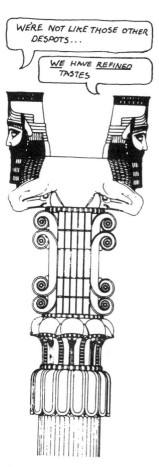

The stylised arrangement of column bases, fluted shafts and flower-like capitals probably derived from primitive buildings constructed of unmodified materials.

The Persians, who had absorbed Assyria into the Persian Empire (until 331 BC), built vast palaces, using stone and marble, with great refinement of detail.

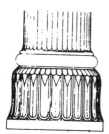

GREECE

Between 3000 and 700 BC, civilisation spread westwards along the Mediterranean to Asia Minor, Greece, Sicily and Southern Italy.

The topography of Greece is characterised by mountains, islands and sea encouraging the evolution of self-contained city states dependent on maritime trade. A sunny temperate climate promoted an outdoor life.

On the island of Crete the Minoan civilisation was based as much on trade as dictatorship; its rulers included merchant princes as well as priest kings. Their palaces had workshops and factories for producing goods for export, especially pottery, and they attracted craft workers from abroad.

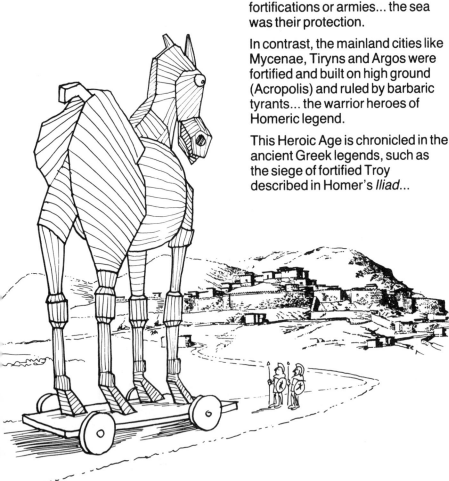

There was no need for fortifications or armies... the sea was their protection.

In contrast, the mainland cities like Mycenae, Tiryns and Argos were fortified and built on high ground (Acropolis) and ruled by barbaric tyrants... the warrior heroes of Homeric legend.

This Heroic Age is chronicled in the ancient Greek legends, such as the siege of fortified Troy described in Homer's *Iliad*...

But in the Iron Age metal technology became more widely available, radically altering society and architecture.

NOW WE CAN REBUILD SOCIETY ACCORDING TO OUR NEEDS

Barbarians, armed with iron weapons, challenged and destroyed the old civilisations which had ruled by means of exclusive bronze technology.

In Greece and Italy a middle class of merchants, financiers and farmer landowners developed. They organised society according to their needs as property owning, free-thinking individuals, and commissioned new building types accordingly.

Culture and religion were adapted to these needs...

EUREKA!

Religion no longer glorified a ruling priest class, but was personalised... the Pantheon of gods was like a family of super humans

Art was no longer in the service of power and religion exclusively, but now became individual and *human*...

Science and Philosophy no longer served the practical requirements of a ruler, but sought to question the natural world objectively. Theory was divorced from practice.

Like so much of western culture, the Greeks virtually *invented* architecture.

The centre of the city-state (the *polis*) was the agora, where political, commercial and cultural activities took place.

Colonnades afforded protection from sun and rain, and the agora would comprise the council chamber, theatre and gymnasium. Temples were located nearby, raised up on an acropolis. Each building was painted in bright colours.

Although religion did not dominate social life it is the temples which have survived as pale ruins to represent Greek civilisation, not the agorae or the spaces *between* buildings.

As in Egypt, the Greek temple evolved from primitive timber POST and LINTEL models.

The orders of which temples were composed have dominated architecture for 2000 years.

There were three Greek orders, each with its own character. They represented **Canonic** (standard) forms to be refined and perfected over generations, combined and varied according to rules, and adjustable to any size or type of building.

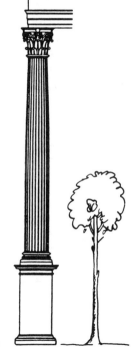

Doric
Symbol of masculine power. The column form probably derived from tooling marks on wooden posts.

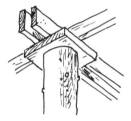

Ionic
Slender and graceful. Female. The capital was based on natural or organic forms — shells or rams' horns.

Corinthian
Tree-like. The capital was reminiscent of acanthus leaves curling round a pot. The least used of the orders.

The Parthenon in Athens, the supreme example of the Doric order, was a public work erected on the Acropolis by the statesman Pericles, chief of the populist party, to celebrate victory over the Persian invaders (and to mop up domestic unemployment).

Greek temples were not designed for congregational worship or as seats of power, but were shrines with spaces in front for sacrifices or ceremonies. They were as much large pieces of sculpture as buildings, and the designers of the Parthenon, Iktinos and Pheidias, were sculptors, builders, *and* architects equally.

Such temples were not built out of pre-formed finished parts. Like sculpture, they were put up in rough stone and finished off by teams of masons.

Early Greek sculpture had been as stiff and lifeless as the Egyptian. Sculptors such as Polykleitos realised that by distorting proportions and emphasising features an impression of life and movement could be conveyed.

The Parthenon too is given "life" by distortion of its parts. It *appears* to be mathematically perfect, with true horizontals and verticals, but this is an illusion.

This unity of architecture and sculpture is well expressed in the Erectheion where statues, Caryatids, hold up the porch.

The buildings on the Acropolis, although individually *symmetrical* (presenting a mirror image each side of a centre line, like the human body) are sited informally (i.e. asymmetrically). It is not clear whether this is simply for effect or for religious reasons. Together they create a constructed natural space.

This unity is also apparent in the huge open-air Greek theatres seemingly formed out of the natural landscape...

PIG!

NOW THAT'S WHAT I CALL DRAMATIC!

OI!

SHE DOESN'T SAY MUCH BUT SHE'S A GREAT SUPPORT

IT'S ALL GREEK TO ME!

31

ROME

The Romans perfected the art of the take-over. First they took over the Etruscans, then they took over Italy and finally they took over the whole world... or what they thought was the whole world... Europe, Asia Minor, North Africa...

Like movie moguls they took over Greek ideas and inflated them into big vulgar productions for the benefit of the state. Colonising became conquering, administration became bureaucracy, and architecture became engineering. Where the separate Greek states imposed their order locally, Roman imperialism steamrollered over whole countries; destroying cultures and imposing its rule by military might, technological superiority, and... architecture.

The Greeks travelled chiefly by sea, in harmony with nature. The Romans drove roads straight as a die across anything in their path, laying waste the landscape on either side to prevent ambush.

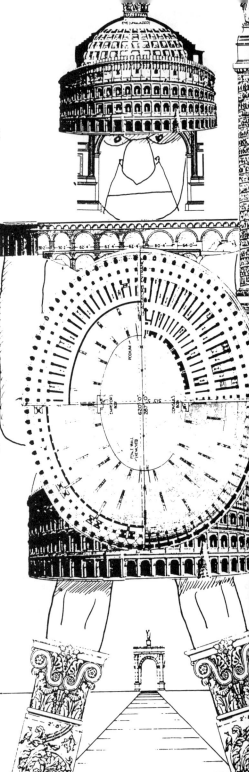

The world was one vast state with Rome at the centre. Each part supported and mirrored the whole.

The centralised fortified city was laid out on a rectangular grid of streets based on military camp planning, symbolic of law and order.

Buildings were equally directional in character, with emphatic fronts and closed-in sides and backs.

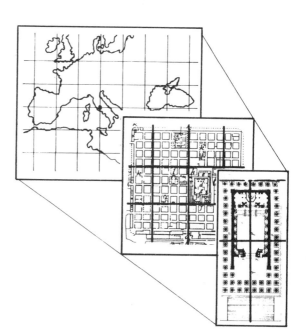

At the centre of the city was the forum; not informal and open like the Greek agora, but enclosed and regular, with colonnades of shops, temples and a basilica (a kind of town hall-cum-law court-cum-stock exchange) forming a protected inward-looking square.

The size of the Greek arch and lintel was limited by the length a single piece of stone can span...

But an arch is made up of small pieces of stone or brick on a wooden framework (centering) which is then removed...

An arch can be as big as you like. All you need are a few thousand slaves to build it.

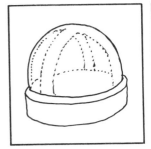

Arches can be combined to form continuous roofs (BARREL VAULTS)... or domes.

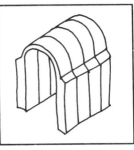

The problem with the arch is that it tends to spread sideways. This has to be countered with thick walls.

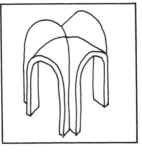

The Romans solved this by combining four vaults into the GROIN VAULT, where each supported the other and allowed large window openings.

The Romans' invention of concrete enabled them to erect massive engineering structures — aqueducts, triumphal arches, public baths or temples — often with the classical orders stuck on to the outside or piled up on top of each other, as in the Colosseum.

The Roman architect was usually a military engineer, but the best known to us is Vitruvius who methodically set down rules for creating architecture using the five orders, the basis for rule books for centuries to come.

ROMAN ARCHITECTURE IS BUILT ON THE PRINCIPLES OF COMMODITY FIRMNESS, DELIGHT ...

... AND SLAVERY !

EARLY CHRISTIAN...

While Rome perfected the take-over, Christianity developed the merger. As the Roman economy disintegrated, owing to its reliance on slavery, the Empire was threatened from without by hordes of barbarian vandals, and from within by... the Christians.

"One God, one Religion, one Church" replaced "one Emperor, one Ideal, one State" as the new international system.
In the West, Christians took over not the Romans' pagan temples but their basilicas. These long halls with colonnades of pillars forming aisles on either side, were ideal for congregational worship. The rounded end where the Roman judge had sat became the APSE in which the altar was placed. New churches were modelled on the basilicas, often incorporating columns quarried from abandoned Roman buildings.

THE DIRECTION IS HORIZONTAL REFLECTING THE WESTERN NOTION OF TIME AS MOVEMENT, CHANGE, PROGRESS, RENEWAL

... BYZANTINE
400 – 1200 AD

ER ... PERHAPS WE COULD COME TO SOME ARRANGEMENT?

As the Roman Empire crumbled, Christianity strengthened. But Christianity needed Rome and Rome needed Christianity in the face of the barbarian threat. A merger was arranged in which Christianity took over the centralised Roman administration.

When things got too hot the Emperor moved the capital to Byzantium (renamed Constantinople), leaving the Pope to hold the fort in Rome.

In the East, Christianity adapted the centralised and domed Roman temple for its church. But space was now required for a congregation looking towards the altar. By the invention of the PENDENTIVE it was possible to sit a dome on a square and the two forms, Roman temple and Christian congregational space, also merged.

. YOU CARRY ON
E ... I'LL HANDLE
EASTERN
R ... OK?

BYZANTIUM

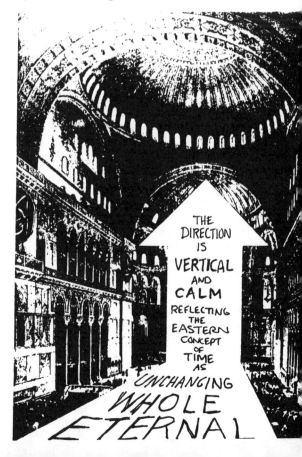

THE DIRECTION IS VERTICAL AND CALM REFLECTING THE EASTERN CONCEPT OF TIME AS UNCHANGING WHOLE ETERNAL

ROMANESQUE 8th – 12th Century

Having first merged with the old Roman Empire and then taken it over, the Christian Church did the same with the Barbarians. Charlemagne, leader of the Franks, was appointed Holy Roman Emperor in AD 800.

Together, Pope and Emperor divided Europe into separate countries, each ruled by their agents, kings (to defend the land and protect the Church) and bishops.

As Church and Barbarians united centrally and locally, so new buildings combined Roman forms (arches, domes) with local building methods and materials adapted to local climates.

Monastic churches used the Roman basilica model with side altars added, forming a cross on plan, and an enlarged west end to accommodate the laity. The main body of the church (NAVE) was occupied by the monks.

Instead of a timber roof the early churches employed either the stone Roman BARREL VAULT or the dome, stone being more permanent and fire proof.

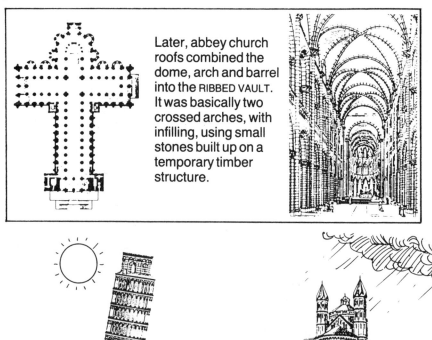

Later, abbey church roofs combined the dome, arch and barrel into the RIBBED VAULT. It was basically two crossed arches, with infilling, using small stones built up on a temporary timber structure.

The Church maintained its power through the monasteries.

The Lord's CASTLE developed by the Normans was an equally exclusive world. At its centre stood a tower (KEEP) with living areas on several levels, surrounded by a wall (BAILEY).

GOTHIC

As the Roman Church gained total control of Europe, its power was expressed through an architecture which exalted its triumph, the **Gothic.**

Gothic developed in a small area in Paris, the Ile de France, during the 11th and 12th Centuries. The French monarch had become rich and powerful and the Pope's main ally.

The growth of royal power and the growth of towns coincided as the king sold land to influential townsmen in return for support in face of threats from the aristocracy. As the king's power grew he needed an educated administration, and since education was monopolised by the Church, bishops became powerful at court. They built large new churches — Gothic cathedrals — on land given by the king.

Gothic symbolised a new synthesis of Humanity, God and Nature. Previously God had been thought of as an unknown and terrible force. Romanesque churches reflected this in their darkness and mystery. Decoration was often grotesque and surreal — strange serpents or devils.
Representations made people identical, their features unimportant.

But now Church scholars in the new cathedral-based universities believed that God revealed himself in His creations, in people and in nature. The Church building became an image of nature, imitating plant forms, ribs, stems or fronds, and growing out of the earth like a tree. Statues were now recognisable portraits of individuals.

The Gothic system exploited three new elements, the POINTED ARCH, the FLYING BUTTRESS and the RIBBED VAULT. Masons had discovered that a pointed arch could be steep or shallow as required.

In the Gothic system the heavy Romanesque walls disappear. The roof is carried via bridges (flying buttresses) to free standing walls at right angles outside.

Stone technology was continually refined and honed by trial and error into an architecture of tension, rhythm and equilibrium, where columns and tracery became as slender as plants and as delicate as lace.

The whole of the Cathedral was a teaching and propaganda tool: an image of Heaven on Earth, a Heavenly City both inside and out.

The west entrance front pictured the Gate into Heaven, usually incorporating sculptures of the Last Judgement, Christ and the Apostles, the Good Souls and the Damned. The sides were also covered in sculptures depicting the temporal world, and like Greek temples, the whole was originally multicoloured.

As with the Romanesque, the Gothic was adapted to local climates and conditions. Rainwater was thrown off the steep roofs by spouts carved into grotesque beasts (GARGOYLES).

Internally the strong vertical lines of structure divided up the space like a mathematical diagram or musical rhythm, representing God's ordering of humanity and nature. Above was the Vault of Heaven, lit from small windows over the nave.

Because of the slender structure large windows were possible, and these were filled with stained glass pictures of light. Light had a special meaning: God, beauty and light (or enlightenment) were one.

Cathedrals had architects, contractors and clients but they were all the same people... the monks, with the same ideals and language. Money was raised through the sale of relics and indulgences to the common people, who might also work as labourers on the buildings.

MEDIEVAL TOWNS

With the expansion of the towns, a new society evolved alongside that of the feudal countryside. International maritime trade returned and towns sited on rivers or estuaries, like Venice, Genoa and Pisa in Italy (the gateways to trade with the East) and Antwerp in the North, grew rapidly.

Merchants, aldermen and landowners were given Royal Charters to set up autonomous local government. Craftworkers and merchants formed guilds to fix prices and control standards.

(Eventually they also took control of local politics.)

Cathedrals became more and more splendid as the style became refined and highly decorated. But absolute power was corrupting the Church — the study of classical texts and the invention of printing were soon to challenge its authority.

This growing challenge could be seen in architecture, where the merchant princes used their wealth and power to erect large urban buildings other than churches or castles… Gothic town halls, guild halls, market halls or colleges.

Venice grew rich on trade with the East. The city's princely ruler, the Doge, built a palace in the 14th Century in a flamboyant Gothic style with Eastern influences.

Members of the Stonemasons' guild were not tied to any one town but could hawk their expertise around. Their guilds guarded the secrets of the masons, the most vital being the ability to construct large buildings from small drawings.

There was no fixed standard measure.

Dimensions had to be transferred from drawing to building by using a method of proportion

— scaling off the drawing with a compass and multiplying it on the building material.

Master masons were sculptors as well as builders, and often the architects of the cathedral or church.

In the North, Flanders was well-positioned to take advantage of both sea routes and farming. Here the cloth trade quickly expanded, with wool brought from England.

HERE WE OPERATE THE GOLDEN FLEECE!

THE VERNACULAR

In spite of their life of drudgery (or because of it) workers and peasants evolved their own counter-cultures, languages, ballads and crafts.

This alternative vernacular culture was also expressed in building. For centuries the homes of ordinary people were built by their inhabitants, or by local builders, using ancient methods, primitive tools and crude materials.

In Northern areas the most important element of the house would be the fireplace and chimney — for warmth and cooking. This would have to be built in stone or local brick, an expensive luxury.

The structure would be formed from roughly hewn curved branches with straight pieces fixed at right angles — like an upturned boat.

The roof might be covered with bundles of dried straw (THATCH) tied on in layers.

For the walls, spaces between the timbers were filled with a mesh of sticks plastered with mud or clay (WATTLE AND DAUB).

Windows were luxury items. Those who could afford it would have a small iron window made by the local smith with bottle glass fixed in with strips of lead. This was such an expensive possession that the owners might take it with them when they moved.

The finished house was simple but effective. Its form was a direct response to the climate and it was built of local ''natural'' materials — timber from the woods, clay from the earth and reeds from the river.

47

THE RENAISSANCE

European kings were now richer and more powerful than Church or nobility, hiring armies and running their countries like big businesses. Taxes were insufficient to finance royal enterprises, such as voyages of discovery to colonise and exploit the New World, so money (capital) had to be borrowed.

In the Italian city state of Florence, money-lending developed into banking. Big bankers, like the Medici family, ran the town, appointed themselves princes and patronised the arts, vying with each other in splendour and ostentation. They demanded buildings which symbolised their mercantile power, and they looked back to the period when Italy was great — the Roman era — for a model. The study of the classical world was given practical application in the new Italian power centres, and classical culture was reborn (Renaissance).

Architects did not merely copy Roman temples or villas; they employed the basic language of classical architecture creatively. Building technology had developed in the Gothic/guild period and now merged with classical principles to produce a new architecture — delicate and ordered. Pattern books of classical designs helped spread the Renaissance throughout Europe.

Although they knew little of ancient Rome, and still less of Greece, Florentine architects believed they were re-creating classical culture. In fact they were continuing the Romanesque style, of which there were many examples in Florence.

Florentine bankers expanded their medieval town houses into palaces, now adorned with classical elements: arched windows, floors defined by horizontal bands (STRING COURSES) and large overhanging moulded tops (CORNICES) hiding the roof. Unlike Roman villas these palaces were urban, located in dangerous narrow streets and consequently aggressive and fortress-like externally. They have served as a model for street architecture ever since.

Internally, though, the palace had a quite different character. A central court with arcades gave light and air to the rooms, comprising service areas on the ground floor and living accommodation on the first (the PIANO NOBILE). Once the street door was bolted, the palace provided a haven from the hostile city outside.

Renaissance architects were not builders but scholars or artists, working out their personal visions through drawings. They were not constrained by guilds but "free" to sell their "genius" to the highest bidder. The Renaissance gave birth to the *superstar* — architect/artist/writer/scientist — the Universal Man.

Brunelleschi (1377–1446) was the first Renaissance Superstar. Goldsmith, sculptor, clockmaker, architect and mathematician, he studied Roman ruins and used this knowledge to win the competition for the design of a dome to complete the Gothic cathedral in Florence.

Brunelleschi combined Roman and Gothic technology in a Byzantine/half-melon form made up of two domes one inside the other, the inner supporting the outer. Metal reinforcing bands between them prevented the outer one spreading.

In Brunelleschi's new buildings, like the Pazzi chapel or Foundling Hospital, the Renaissance style proper was born. Neither Classical nor Gothic, it dominated Western architecture for 500 years. Brunelleschi took the elements of Roman building — the wall, columns, arches, pediments, cornices — and composed new spaces where the outside and inside were integrated and unified in harmony and proportion.

Classical orders and elements were used by Renaissance architects both internally and externally like a variable kit of parts…

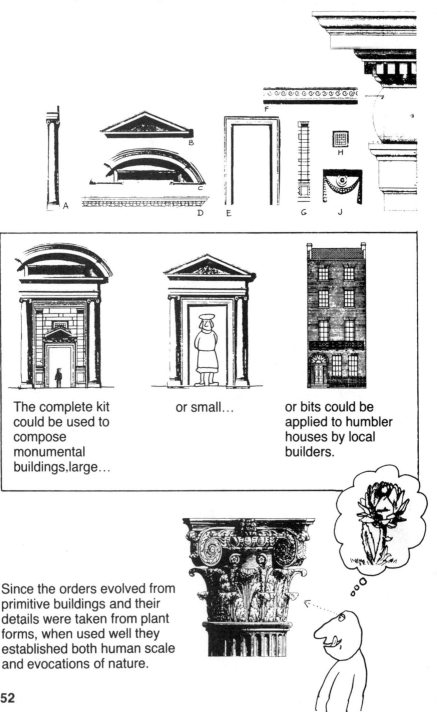

The complete kit could be used to compose monumental buildings, large…

or small…

or bits could be applied to humbler houses by local builders.

Since the orders evolved from primitive buildings and their details were taken from plant forms, when used well they established both human scale and evocations of nature.

Another superstar, Leone Battista Alberti (1404–72), developed theories of PROPORTION which equated beauty with geometry.

Taking his cue from Vitruvius, he related the human body to the square and the circle — "perfect" forms in the image of God and Nature. Alberti argued that buildings too should be composed according to the same divine laws of harmony — the basic forms were to be double squares and double cubes — enhanced by ornament (on everything from candelabra to columns). As in music, buildings should be a balance of harmonious parts, nothing could be added or subtracted.

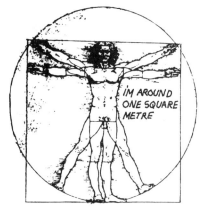

IM AROUND ONE SQUARE METRE

Alberti's few buildings involved the completion of existing churches, such as Santa Maria Novella in Florence. Here parts of the old Gothic front were beautifully combined with Renaissance elements using the laws of proportion to make a balanced composition. However, as with the Parthenon, this was probably achieved more by eye than by ruler.

I LIKE TO KEEP A SENSE OF PROPORTION !

MANNERISM 16th Century

Just as Gothic architecture had become more decorated, the High Renaissance of the 16th Century was bolder, more confident and sculptural. In Mannerism, the classical rules were bent, distorted, juggled and eventually almost entirely dispensed with. The Orders were employed in free compositions and individual statements, particularly in church design. Stars of this phase were Bramante (1444–1514), Michelangelo (1475–1504), Vignola (1507–1573) and Palladio (1508–1580).

Whereas Gothic churches had evolved to meet the requirements of the liturgy — nave for congregation, apse for altar — Renaissance architects believed that plans should be based purely on geometrical shapes — squares, circles, crosses — to reflect natural harmony, with man at the centre. In a church designed on a centralised plan, though, where do the altar and congregation go? This conflict between architectural theory and practical requirements has been with us ever since.

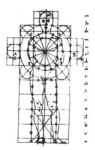

St Peters in Rome was started by Bramante and Michelangelo as a Greek Cross, but the Church insisted on a nave being added, which made the church enormous in scale and awkward internally. Michelangelo added the dome (following Brunelleschi's technology) and the front façade.

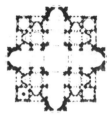

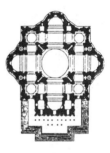

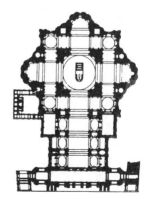

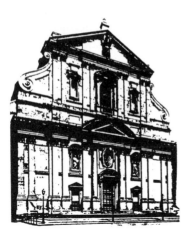

This problem was solved by Vignola in the Church of Il Gesu in Rome, which served as a model for Renaissance churches for years after. The Gesu was the base of the Jesuits, leaders of the Counter Reformation. Just as they set about promoting the old religion with new techniques, so their church cleverly combined the centralised and longtitudinal plans. To amplify the message, aisles and arms were turned into side chapels.

The front employs all the Mannerist tricks: columns of different heights, curved pediments inside triangular ones, scrolls and niches among them.

Andrea Palladio had the greatest influence of any Renaissance architect, principally due to his Four Books on the theory and practice of design. He also advocated a return to a cool, refined classical architecture designed according to the laws of Nature and the order of the universe as embodied in mathematical proportion. But his designs were simple and practical and extended the idea of the building reflecting the elements of the human body (biomorphism):

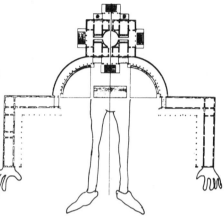

★ The building should be symmetrical (the left half mirrors the right) around an axis (the spine) from the front, but not from the side.

★ Each part should relate to the whole and to every other part. The more important elements are in the middle (head, brain, eyes etc).

★ Elements on the outside should reflect the structure inside (the skin over bones).

Palladio designed a series of country villas for the landed gentry around Venice according to these principles. He assumed that Roman villas had been like small temples so he attached temple fronts to the traditional rural farm house model while integrating the building into its landscape setting.

THE REFORMATION 16th Century

By the 16th Century the centre of banking and trade had moved from Italy to Germany and the Netherlands.

The Pope still had influence, but keeping up with kings was expensive. Finance for huge projects like St Peter's was raised by selling indulgences, fake relics or positions in high places. In Germany, the new urban rich objected to the Church's influence — it hampered business. Prompted by this and the Church's corruption, parts of the German Church severed themselves from Rome to pursue their own brands of Christianity. Protestantism was born. This revolt, nourished by the printed word, spread throughout the North.

Science, struggling to free itself from the Church's control, sought to study facts and formulate laws as in Ancient Greece. Industry was becoming increasingly regionalised and work specialised.

In the North, the Renaissance first took the form of classical elements grafted on to local Gothic structural forms, symbolising the encroachment of the new culture on to the old.

NEW CHATEAU — OLD CHAPEAU !

France's invasions of Italy exposed it to Renaissance art. The French aristocracy's châteaux in the Loire valley slowly absorbed the Classical style. But while they were no longer fortified castles, they still maintained medieval corner towers, turrets, and high pitched roofs.

HARDWICK HALL, MORE GLASS THAN WALL !

Equally, in England, which had grown into a world power during Elizabeth's reign, aristocrats built huge country houses which combined Medieval, Classical and Flemish elements. Gigantic windows, first developed in Gothic cathedrals, were added, symbols of both the transfer of power from Church to laity and their confidence in the stability of the new social order.

THE BAROQUE 17th Century

In the 17th Century, France emerged as the most powerful state, centralised under an Absolute Monarch with a self-proclaimed Divine Right to rule. The King *was* the state. Not only business but the arts and sciences were regulated by the King through newly-formed Academies. A new breed of architects was spawned — the official court adviser who designed palaces, public buildings and churches for the state. For these monuments of vast scale and cost the appropriate style flourished... Baroque.

While Mannerism played games with the Orders, the Baroque subordinated them to the expression of a simple, unified dynamic concept. This extended far beyond buildings to include the surrounding landscape or townscape. Modern TOWN PLANNING was born.

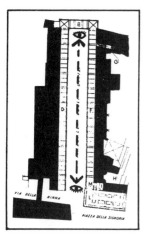

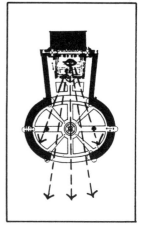

Renaissance
architects' perception of space was altered by the rules of perspective. The Uffizi palace in Florence is a group of buildings linking two parts of the old city, designed to be seen from one viewpoint.

Mannerism
developed this idea of renewing part of a town. In Michelangelo's Campidoglio in Rome, the composition is designed to change, when seen from different viewpoints both inside looking out or inside looking in.

Baroque planning exploits time and space. Usually planned on a vast scale, its long vistas give an illusion of infinity and endlessly change as you move through them. Bernini added a piazza in front of St Peter's according to these principles.

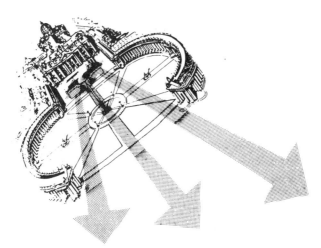

Baroque planning and absolute monarchy went hand in hand, but in architecture the finest expression of the Baroque is to be found in ecclesiastical buildings.

- During the Renaissance period architecture was essentially static.
- It was composed of separate and defined elements according to the laws of proportion.
- Flat walls expressed simple geometric plans.
- The Baroque developed from Mannerism into a dynamic and unified architecture.
- Classical elements were integrated with sculpture, distorted and manipulated for dramatic effect.
- Undulating walls did not always relate to complex plans.

The oval is a typical Baroque form. In church plans it integrated the rectangle and the circle to achieve simultaneous directional and centralised space, fulfilling the aims of architects and clergy alike.

To counter the Reformation, Italy embarked on a church building programme to promulgate anew the old religion. These churches exploited Baroque decoration and ostentation as a deliberate contrast to Protestant austerity.

In Rome the principal architects of the Baroque were the rivals Bernini (1589–1680) flamboyant courtier, politician and sculptor, and Borromini (1599–1667) fanatic, introvert, anarchist.

Their two best known churches, both based on oval plans, express the contrast in their personalities.

San Carlo by Borromini (left) unifies its classical based elements in a revolutionary manner by fusing them into an undulating, flowing plastic, whole.

San Andrea (right) by Bernini confidently employs classical elements and manipulates their scale to achieve an integration of sculpture, painting and architecture, like a stage set.

Stars of the Baroque in France were, among others, the Mansards — uncle François (1598-1666) who adopted the steep North French roof and applied it to classical-style buildings, and nephew Hardouin (1648-1708), Le Vau (1612-1670), and le Notre (1613-1700).

The last three were all official architects for Louis XVII's vast palace at Versailles. A quarter of a mile long, it has endless formal gardens at the rear where long intersecting paths extend outwards to infinity.

It symbolised the King's total power over nation and nature. Versailles housed the seat of government, the court and high society.

INFINITE POWER –
INFINITE SPACE

PLAN GENERAL
DES
VILLE et CHATEAU
DE VERSAILLES

In England the King had to share power with Parliament, so when Charles I tried to play the Absolute Monarch, civil war ensued. The King's trial and decapitation took place at the Banqueting Hall, designed by the architect Inigo Jones. Jones (1573–1652), a follower of Palladio, believed buildings should be masculine — disciplined and without affectation. His quiet, serene classicism was to have a great effect in England.

The Baroque style was eventually adopted by the Protestant Church in northern countries. In Germany and Austria there was a flurry of church and monastery building after the exhausting 30 years war. Outstanding figures included J.M. Fischer (1692–1766) von Hildebrandt (1668–1745) and Neuman (1687–1753).

With the Restoration of the monarchy and renewed affluence, England had a period of restrained Baroque, led by some outstanding court architects, Christopher Wren (1632–1723), John Vanbrugh (1664–1776) and Nicholas Hawkesmoor (1661–1736).

Wren, an astronomer and mathematician, designed many churches in the rebuilding of London after the Great Fire (1666), the best-known being St Paul's Cathedral.

IF YOU SEEK HIS MONUMENT LOOK ABOUT YOU

While Catholic churches were focussed on the altar, and expressed the mystery of the ceremony, Protestants required a large space for people to gather — the sermon and Bible reading were as important as the service, the pulpit as important as the altar. But when Wren, like Michelangelo, wanted to build a centralised, domed church, he too came into conflict with his patron. The Protestant clergy insisted on retaining the separation of priest and congregation by including a nave. Although he was forced to compromise, Wren still managed to make his dome dominate his restrained Baroque composition.

THE EAST

China

The static nature of ancient Chinese society did not foster monumental buildings; famous landmarks such as the Great Wall, built to keep out invading barbarians, or the Forbidden City, are rather transformations of the environment using water, earth and space in which buildings are incidentals.

RAIN PRESSES DOWN ON WHAT IS
COVERED,
BUT WHAT IS OPEN LETS IT THROUGH.
UNCOVER THEREFORE WHAT IS COVERED,
AND SO THE RAIN WILL DO NO HARM.

For centuries, China was ruled by the Emperor and a large bureaucracy which controlled every aspect of life from trade to religion. Sizes and types of houses were strictly controlled according to class. There was no hereditary aristocracy or wealthy merchants to build grand palaces or castles.

Small, delicate, linked elements — gateways, bridges, walkways — sited in accordance with ancient magic principles relating to nature, typify traditional Chinese architecture.

Not until Buddhism and its temples were introduced from India did any idea of permanence or posterity intrude into the eastern notion of time as a whole entity.

Chinese architecture is the architecture of the roof, supported on a timber post-and-beam structure, tiled and steeply sloping to throw off the rain, with upward curving overhanging eaves affording protection from the sun, while reflecting diffused light into the interior.

Japan

Japanese architecture, like Japanese society, was influenced by China — yet was lighter, more delicate and refined. Buildings were also built with timber frames to survive earthquakes. Framed structures are more flexible and can cope with movement (in contrast to heavy masonry).

The Buddhist pagoda came from China via India and west Asia and consists of roofs piled up around a central post akin to tree forms. Again, like a tree, such a structure is designed to cope with earth movement.

The traditional Japanese house, developed from the house for the Tea Ceremony, is made up of a series of mats of standard size with light, simple modular walls of black frame and white infill panels. These can be slid open to connect inside and outside spaces.

Chinese, and particularly Japanese, architecture had a great influence on the West, especially on 19th Century England and on the work of Frank Lloyd Wright in 20th Century America.

THE AGE OF REASON 18th Century

In most of the powerful states of 18th Century Europe, wealth and government were in the hands of an Absolute Monarch and the aristocracy.

The growing middle class increasingly resented royal power and its vast expenditure on war and armies. It limited their freedom to make money.

SLUMS, RICH, POOR, DISEASE... THERE'S A PERFECTLY *RATIONAL* EXPLANATION FOR IT ALL!

In France, with its tradition of large architectural scale, Boullée (1728–1799) made Roman-inspired drawings of massive geometric monuments to cult figures like... Newton.

NATURE AND NATURE'S LAWS LAY HID IN NIGHT, GOD SAID: LET NEWTON BE! AND ALL WAS LIGHT

It was an age of "Reason". Science was thought to be able to measure everything from art and religion to the principle of Absolutism itself. Newton had shown that even the mysteries of the universe were subject to the laws of science. Taste in all things became simple, refined, rational.

Architecture, reacting to Baroque excesses, looked once more to Greek and Roman models. Neo-classicism, with its clear rules and principles, was appropriate to "rational" taste.

In England, the refined taste makers followed Palladio. The Palladians were gentlemen architects designing neo-classical Venetian villas for the English landed aristocracy…

… But a different patron was now emerging, the new middle class. If they could not afford individual Palladian palaces, entrepreneurial architects fulfilled their aspirations for taste and privilege by designing town houses joined together in terraces to give an overall impression of a grand palatial building.

REVOLUTION

The bourgeois revolutions in America and France at the end of the 18th Century laid the foundations for the modern world ... and for **modern architecture**. British imperialism in America and absolute monarchy in France were repressive obstacles to the expansion of free market capitalism. After the revolution everyone had the Liberty and Equality to join the Fraternity of self-made capitalists.

The revolutions were equally products of the Age of Reason and their architecture reverted to classical purity and order.

> THE NEW ROME

The Capitol, the Triumphal Arch and the Pantheon... were the models for the monuments glorifying the new democratic republics.

> THE NEW ATHENS

THE WORKSHOP OF THE WORLD...

The main impetus to capitalism in England was the Industrial Revolution, the change from handcraft to machine mass production in factories.

This revolution also developed from the Age of Reason and the quest for knowledge about the physical world. Inventors, entrepreneurs and industrialists competed in a *laissez-faire* economy devoid of controls, making fortunes from mass production using cheap labour and raw materials from the Empire.

In a short space of time great areas of the country were altered... to the unacceptable face of capitalism. Railways smashed through old towns and cities to serve factories, spewing pollution, noise, ugliness and disease over the whole community. The Age of Reason had in the name of Progress produced an environment more inhuman than any previously in history.

Driven off the land, their guilds abolished and rights taken away, the rural poor flocked to the towns for work; to be crammed into quickly erected back-to-back houses without sanitation, water or ventilation and subject to the noise and smoke from the adjacent factory. They came in three grades, semi-slum, slum and super slum.

Yet somehow in the face of these terrible conditions a community spirit of mutual help and support often developed in the mean cobbled streets.

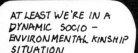

AT LEAST WE'RE IN A DYNAMIC SOCIO-ENVIRONMENTAL KINSHIP SITUATION

And what were the architects doing…?

As usual they went where the money was, servicing the new rich's desire for respectability and taste by dressing up their mansions, town halls and offices in any historical style they chose… Gothic, Renaissance, Baroque, Egyptian, you name it, architects could provide it. Architects formed professional closed shops to fix fees and stop undercutting amateurs from getting their hands on the new source of loot.

But the political and industrial revolutions were to change the face of architecture fundamentally.

As well as Rationalism in art there were now other isms. Romanticism looked directly to nature for inspiration; while Nationalism sought to promote indigenous characteristics in opposition to the imported "foreign" classicism of the old regimes. Pugin (1812–1852) for example, saw Gothic not merely as a style, but as the one true, honest, natural, democratic, free *English* architecture (although it had of course originated in France); and led the way to the **Gothic Revival**.

Architectural style was now seen as the embodiment of moral and political values.

In his book "True Principles of Pointed or Christian Architecture", Pugin set down his rules for an architecture of TRUTH:

● Nothing must be included which was not for "convenience, construction or propriety." The building must honestly express its function and materials.

● Ornament should consist of "the essential construction of the building". The structure must be expressed not covered up with arbitrary or superflous decoration.

The expansion of Great Britain and its empire in the 19th century fired a reaction to the dominance of Greece and Rome and a desire to revert to its Nordic roots.

In England the aristocracy was more flexible in the exercise of power and able to absorb the emerging middle class industrialists (along with their wealth) into existing institutions, even giving them the vote in 1832.

When the new Houses of Parliament were built in 1835 they combined a formal neo-classical plan by one architect (Charles Barry) with Gothic Revival façades by another (Pugin), nicely symbolising the marriage of the old establishment with the new money.

The bourgeois state now required its own buildings… government administration centres, prisons, museums etc.
In France there was a move to break with the architectural tradition of the old regimes, not to imitate past styles but to create new forms for new functions. Le Doux (1736–1806), like Boullée, was inspired by late Roman monumental engineering…

19th Century ENGINEERING

Iron had been used in buildings for centuries in the form of door handles, window frames or fixings, usually beaten out by the local smith. But the discovery of smelting iron ore using coke in a blast furnace meant that large quantities of standard components could be cast in moulds and mass-produced to make not only machines but structural members also. Stronger, more fire-resistant and durable than timber, they could, in addition, be erected more quickly.

Engineers replaced architects as inventors of imaginative structures. Using mass-produced iron (and later steel) components they designed new structures, undreamed of before, to house the industrialists' machines, railway stations, docks, factories, bridges, exhibition halls, museums...

WE CAN NOW DO THE IMPOSSIBLE — MIRACLES TAKE A LITTLE LONGER

1851 and display products of Britain and her Empire. Paxton was the archetypal self-made man, uneducated and uncultured but endowed with a brilliantly inventive mind. By observing the structure of the leaf he had developed a greenhouse design using standard iron and glass elements. The Crystal Palace design evolved from this, but on a vast scale.

It took only six months to make and erect the components and it was the wonder of the age (except to architects). Internally a seemingly never-ending, barely-enclosed space — it was a fitting symbol of the free and unlimited possibilities for British capitalism and imperialism.

One of the best known engineering structures of the 19th Century was the Crystal Palace designed by Joseph Paxton to house the Great Exhibition of

ARTS AND CRAFTS

But there were those who detested the Crystal Palace, not because of snobbery, but for what it contained and stood for. Two critics of the over-decorated, machine mass produced objects displayed were John Ruskin (1819–1900) and William Morris (1834–1896). Ruskin and Morris had been influenced both by Pugin and the Gothic Revivalists and Rousseau's romantic notion of primitive man, as well as new ideas about the role of the artist which developed after the second French revolution of 1848. Revolutionary artists demanded an art in the service of the people, by the people and for the people… supporting the revolution against the privileged élite who had previously been their patrons.

THE ARCHITECT IS CAREFULLY GUARDED FROM THE COMMON TROUBLES OF THE COMMON MAN, BUILDING FOR IGNORANT, PURSE PROUD DIGESTING MACHINES… LIVING **ART** MUST HAVE MORE IN IT THAN IMITATED **STYLE** …

THE GREAT CRY THAT RISES FROM ALL OUR MANUFACTURING CITIES, LOUDER THAN THEIR FURNACE BLAST, IS… THAT WE MANUFACTURE EVERYTHING THERE EXCEPT **MEN**… TO BRIGHTEN, TO STRENGTHEN, TO REFINE OR TO FORM A SINGLE LIVING **SPIRIT**, NEVER ENTERS INTO OUR ESTIMATE OF ADVANTAGES

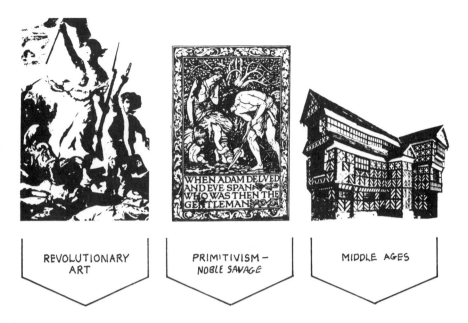

REVOLUTIONARY ART

PRIMITIVISM — NOBLE SAVAGE

MIDDLE AGES

For Morris and Ruskin, classical architecture was both foreign *and* the imposition of ruling class taste on society. Horrified by the effects of the Industrial Revolution, they looked back to the Middle Ages when they felt workers had pride in their craft and were not slaves to the machine and capitalism. Morris went further. He proclaimed that if architecture was as important as cultured people said, it should be accessible to everybody and not just to the élite. He wanted architects to turn their attentions away from historic styles and tackle the terrible inhuman environment created by the Industrial Revolution.

Morris was not against the machine as such, so long as it was used for society's benefit, and not to enslave the work force.

Architecture for the people should draw inspiration not from classical Italian palazzi, but from the people's own buildings, the simple homes and churches of rural England. In his view these were as worthy of the name Architecture as the grand monuments. For Morris they were in fact *more* worthy, being honest, truly English, appropriate to the climate and built of natural, untreated materials.

I HAVE HOPE THAT IT WILL BE FROM SUCH NECESSARY, UNPRETENTIOUS BUILDINGS THAT THE NEW AND GENUINE ARCHITECTURE WILL SPRING, RATHER THAN FROM EXPERIMENTS IN CONSCIOUS STYLE

The Red House near London of 1859 was designed for Morris and his circle of Pre-Raphaelite friends by the young architect Philip Webb to express all their ideas about a new, free architecture inspired by native buildings.

Today the Red House looks like a slightly austere, typically Victorian house, but when it was built it caused a sensation. It was thought shocking that "cultured" artists should attempt to ape the "crude" buildings of the lower orders. Modern Architecture was born.

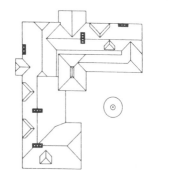

DO WHAT IS CONVENIENT; AND IF THE FORM BE A NEW ONE, SO MUCH THE BETTER
Ruskin

NEO CLASSIC

Rational

The house was designed from the inside. Instead of starting with a symmetrical front and fitting the rooms in behind (classical), each room was considered in terms of its view and light. Most rooms faced north as they were to double as artists' studios.

National

The materials were not imported marble but local red brick and tile, timber was left natural and untreated inside.

The house like vernacular buildings, mixed diverse elements — turrets, Gothic pointed arches, Georgian windows.

Romantic

Instead of cutting all the trees down to make a flat table to show off the building the house is built *amidst* the trees on an orchard site in a "natural" rustic way. The well is symbolic of this unity of house and land.

Morris's view of the noble worker was patronising and romantic. Real workers were too busy organising unions to worry about a return to joyful labour. But his ideas were a success with the newly-affluent middle class — they lapped up his craft-based work and the new architecture.

The Arts and Crafts ideals spread throughout the new European democracies, where they drew on each country's own vernacular. Local and national variations developed in opposition to the imperial neo-Classical styles of the old regimes.

The houses of Voysey (1857–1941) represent the perfection of the simple rural style. Economical and carefully detailed, often with whitewashed walls and friendly roofs, they enabled the stockbroker and banker to have the best of both worlds — the simple country life and quick rail link to their city offices.

ART NOUVEAU

As western Europe liberated new nations from old empires there was an end-of-century spirit of leaving behind the old for the *new*... A new democratic society, new industrial prosperity and new Art. Art Nouveau followed the Arts and Crafts movement in rejecting the styles of the old order but not its linking of art to social consciousness and nationalism. It did not look back to some medieval Gothic ideal but forward with the new industrial wealth.

Art Nouveau drew its inspiration direct from nature to create a new style. The free-form curve became its hall mark... the dynamic stem structure of plants and buds rather than flowers... lilies, sunflowers, tree roots, the swan and peacock... anything which symbolised purity, freedom and promise. Art Nouveau combined many influences, especially stylised Japanese art, which had become fashionable with the opening up of trade with the East.

In England the followers of Morris despised the new art for being decadent, élitist and — most hateful of all — done for its own sake rather than in pursuit of some higher social ideal…

But in Europe there was no such division. Art Nouveau architecture developed in Belgium and France to exploit the new possibilities of cast iron. It was an ideal material for shaping into organic curves, fusing structure and decoration as in Guimard's (1867–1942) famous Paris Métro entrances.

L'ART NOUVEAU RICHE!

THE NEW ART IN THE SERVICE OF THE NEW TECHNOLOGY

NOTHING ?!!

AH, MY FREIND YOU'VE FORGOTTEN THE ONE ESSENTIAL INGREDIENT!

LASHINGS OF MONEY… ET VOILA —

In Germany and Austria Art Nouveau's architectural character was more geometric. Otto Wagner (1841–1918) was the father figure of the new Viennese architecture, together with his pupils Olbrich (1867–1908) and Hoffman (1870–1956).

At the end of the century, during the last days of the corrupt Hapsburg empire, Wagner designed a headquarters for the Secession, an alternative to the Vienna academy which would not exhibit the new art. The art gallery, which had moveable partitions, was topped by a golden sphere, a symbol of hope. . .

The purest Art Nouveau architecture can be found in the work of Antonio Gaudí (1852–1926) in Barcelona where the whole building becomes a fusion of organic based form and structure, like a piece of sculpture, incorporating Spanish Baroque and North African influences.

His designs were often statements of nationalism as in the Casa Batllo (1906) which symbolises Catalonia's desire for independence. The roof represents Barcelona's patron saint St George slaying the dragon of Spain. The death mask balconies and bone-like structure symbolise Catalan martyrs.

Another great individual architect, Charles Rennie Mackintosh (1868–1928), worked in Glasgow, a town which at the time enjoyed great industry and wealth. In his School of Art all the new developments come together — Scottish vernacular-inspired Arts and Crafts and Art Nouveau's fusion of structure and decoration through the use of iron and glass. The relation of the building to its steep site and the informal planning combine in a sure and confident exploitation of space heralding a new urban architecture, robust yet delicate in detail, functional yet inspiring and human in scale, economic yet rich in imagination.

I'M HIS WIFE — MARGERET MACDONALD (DESIGNER) IN THE BACKGROUND AS USUAL

Although Mackintosh was recognised as a genius and leader by the Art Nouveau movement in Europe, the British decided they knew better. He did few major buildings after the School of Art and took to the bottle and wallpaper design. For Britain it was the end of the new architecture.

BLOOD AND IRON

Germany, newly unified under the Prussian military aristocracy (the Junkers) rapidly industrialised and outpaced Britain to become the strongest and richest nation in Europe. Military style planning, machine production and land ownership under state control enabled Germany, drawing on massive resources of coal and iron, to develop giant new concerns in the steel, chemicals and electrical industries.

In its search for efficient methods, the German government investigated the new English architecture. In the simplified and relatively unadorned forms, it saw not a source of social reform, but a style that could be adapted for machine production — clean, efficient, economic.

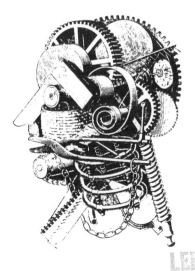

THE ENGLISH HOUSE

Hellman

The Courtship

In Germany, many progressive architects had changed their view of the role of the machine. Rather than resisting it, the machine was now seen as architecture's salvation. With it a new modern architecture appropriate to the 20th Century would be created.

Germany put these ideas into operation.

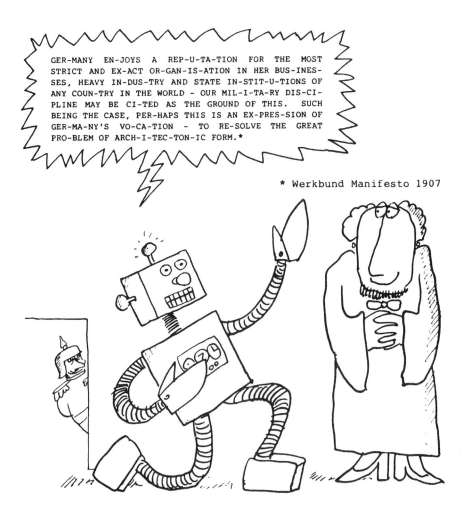

GER-MANY EN-JOYS A REP-U-TA-TION FOR THE MOST STRICT AND EX-ACT OR-GAN-IS-ATION IN HER BUS-INES-SES, HEAVY IN-DUS-TRY AND STATE IN-STIT-U-TIONS OF ANY COUN-TRY IN THE WORLD - OUR MIL-I-TA-RY DIS-CI-PLINE MAY BE CI-TED AS THE GROUND OF THIS. SUCH BEING THE CASE, PER-HAPS THIS IS AN EX-PRES-SION OF GER-MA-NY'S VO-CA-TION - TO RE-SOLVE THE GREAT PRO-BLEM OF ARCH-I-TEC-TON-IC FORM.*

* Werkbund Manifesto 1907

The Marriage

In 1907 a government organisation, the Werkbund, was set up under the direction of the architect Peter Behrens (1868–1940) to bring together industry and designers so that design for mass production would promote both efficiency and the greater glory of the Fatherland. A marriage was arranged between architecture and the machine, and the architectural designs appropriate to the needs of state capitalism were drawn up.

The Honeymoon ....

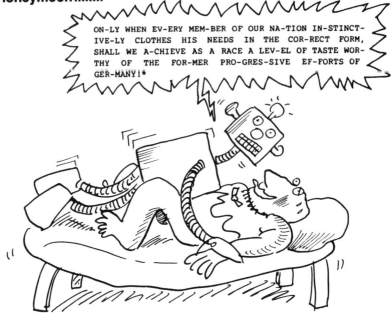

ON-LY WHEN EV-ERY MEM-BER OF OUR NA-TION IN-STINCT-IVE-LY CLOTHES HIS NEEDS IN THE COR-RECT FORM, SHALL WE A-CHIEVE AS A RACE A LEV-EL OF TASTE WOR-THY OF THE FOR-MER PRO-GRES-SIVE EF-FORTS OF GER-MANY!*

* Werkbund Manifesto 1907

The Pregnancy ....

GER-MANY IS IN THE HAP-PY SIT-U-A-TION THAT IT HAS NOT YET SHOWN ITS STRENGTH ... HERE IT IS IN-DEED THE EAR-LY MOR-NING THAT WE EX-PER-IENCE. PER-HAPS THE MID-DAY CAN BE-STOW BEAU-TI-FUL THINGS UPON US.*

The Birth ....

The Machine Aesthetic was born...
the factory as monumental temple.

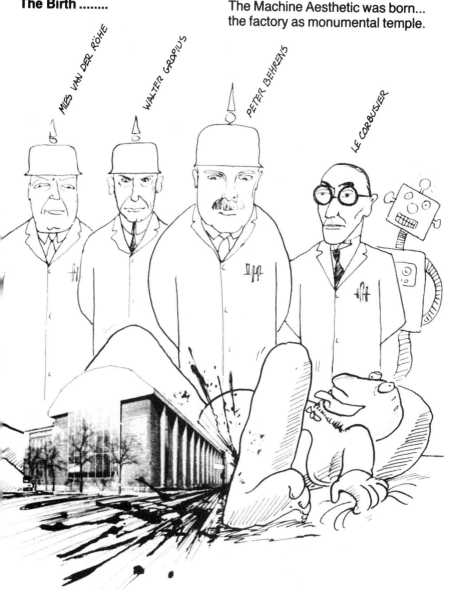

Associated with Behrens and the Werkbund were the young architects who would develop the new Functional Machine style in the 20s and 30s...

Walter Gropius (1883–1969), Mies van der Röhe (1886–1969), Le Corbusier (1887–1966).

STEEL

Walter Gropius, an ex-officer in the Prussian army, was the first to develop the Machine Aesthetic of the future.

By the end of the 19th Century methods of production were developed which enabled steel to be rolled into girders of immense length. Steel, stronger and lighter than iron, soon replaced it for skeleton structures which were then clad on the outside in stone or brick to simulate traditional buildings.

To Gropius, this was "dishonest". In part of the Fagus shoe factory (1911) he designed the whole of the external wall as a glass membrane through which the framed structure could be seen. Here was the sheer, naked, abstract form of the architecture of the future — repetitive, machine-made components housing the very machines that produced them.

EEK! NO CORNER!

AMERICAN GRAIN SILOS... COAL BUNKERS... WORK HALLS BEAR COMPARISON, IN THEIR OVERWHELMING MONUMENTAL POWER, WITH THE BUILDING OF ANCIENT EGYPT

AND GLASS

Historically, buildings like Gothic cathedrals often had large windows. But the idea of the glass wall wrapped around a skeleton frame, was first developed in *parts* of buildings by Gropius, and then as *whole* buildings by Bruno Taut (1880–1938).

In Vienna, the change from Art Nouveau to a harder geometric style is seen in the work of Adolf Loos (1870–1933), the somewhat confused prophet of the Modern Movement. He declared forms inspired by the simplicity and unpretentiousness he found both in engineers' work and peasant homes to be the true Spirit of the Age (*zeitgeist*). Ornament and decoration he equated with barbarism. His best known aphorism was "Ornament is crime."

BRAVE NEW WORLD

By 1914 fierce competition among European capitalist states for economic domination of the world exploded in the First World War. Afterwards it seemed as if the old world of Empires and distinct countries had been swept away for good and the world would be created anew.

Modern architects, adopting their Romantic/Renaissance role of special men apart from society, saw themselves as leaders in the creation of Utopia starting with a clean sheet. Tradition and history could be ignored as irrelevant. The New Order would be determined purely by science and technology.

The traditional language of architecture would be eradicated for good and replaced by functional machine-made forms.

It was felt that architectural and planning problems could be analysed objectively and the correct and only possible "solution" determined through the application of technology. Art and subjectivism could be dispensed with. The designers of buildings would no longer be individual artists but anonymous groups of engineers/technicians.

The idea of Utopia through architecture was fuelled by an equally crude interpretation of the ideas of the architects of the 20th Century: Darwin, Marx, Freud and Einstein.

Einstein's Theory of Relativity demonstrated that the world and universe were not arranged according to some grand fixed master plan but were continually changing and evolving... change was the only certain element. Each person observed the world differently. To the three dimensions of length, height and breadth was added a *fourth*... time.

This consciousness of space and time found expression in the forms of the new architecture which seemed to extend to infinity, the outside walls dissolved into glass. Buildings were given a three dimensional quality which seemed best appreciated when seen from a speeding car or plane...

FUTURISM

A vision of how whole cities would be transformed by the new machine-made world had been drawn up by the Italian Futurist architect Sant Elia (1888–1917) in 1914. Italy, recently unified and just beginning to industrialise, was not inhibited by any industrial tradition. The Futurists did not just accept the machine, they *worshipped* it. Art and architecture would exhibit all the dynamic streamlined qualities of the new aeroplanes, liners, motorcars and motorcycles.

Marx saw history following an inevitable pattern that would lead to the destruction of capitalism and the emergence of a new unalienated human being in a new socialist society.

CONSTRUCTIVISM

For many modern architects Utopia already existed — in the USSR. In the heady anarchic days after the revolution young Soviet architects drew up plans for buildings to express the spirit of the new collective industrial society. This Constructivist style was generally more akin to the dynamic, romantic vision of the Futurists than the stern puritanism of the Werkbund. Unlike the latter this vision was, however, short-lived…

EXPRESSIONISM

Freud was the architect of 20th Century psychological man, no longer ruled by reason applied to external phenomena but (as the Romantics believed) by psychological forces. But now it was thought that these forces could be measured or predicted scientifically by analysis. Analysis employed metaphor and symbolism.

In Germany the Expressionists rejected the hard, rectilinear and "functional" standard boxes of the Werkbund in favour of an individual and romantic approach. Buildings were meant to express or symbolise their use, bringing together form and content in a new personal language. Symbols used were often those relating to speed and machines (boats, pistons) as well as being often consciously or subconsciously sexual.

The best known of this group was another Prussian, Erich Mendelsohn (1887–1953). In 1920 he designed the Einstein tower observatory for Einstein himself. The Functionalists scorned its weird plastic form as sham because it is carved out of brick to imitate concrete.

Above: Dutch Expressionist Volkstheater Project.

FUNCTIONALISM

Darwin had shown that animal behaviour was highly adapted to and conditioned by the environment, so could not the equation be reversed? Provide the "correct" environment, and "correct" behaviour would necessarily evolve. People would be transformed into a higher state of happiness and contentment. For the pioneer modern architects the "correct" environment was the clean, functional, machine-made forms as laid down by the Werkbund. Architects would engineer the society of the future.

The Werkbund hardliners looked back to eras when they felt structure had been expressed honestly, as in Greece and Rome or the Gothic cathedrals. But above all they admired the German neo-Classical architecture of Schinkel. Thus the New Machine Aesthetic merged conveniently with the characteristics of Prussian new-Classicism... repetitious, orderly and anonymous.

Architects like Mies van der Röhe believed they were akin to engineers, designing rational structures free of style. Fulfil the *function* and the *form* will follow automatically. What they actually did was to invent a style that *looked* "rational" — repetitive, austere, mathematical, cold — but was no more the product of objective scientific method than any other architecture.

REINFORCED CONCRETE

The Modern Movement made great claims to being about "truth" to materials. It is ironic then that the main structural material of the 20th Century should be a highly "unnatural" amalgam of two materials... concrete and steel.

The Romans used concrete to construct their massive edifices. With slave labour it was a quick and cheap substitute for stone walls and could be faced in real stone or brick.

A sort of mixture of sandy earth, lime and water was poured into timber moulds...

When set the resulting concrete shape was very tough... in COMPRESSION...

but not...

in TENSION.

Concrete was abandoned until the industrial revolution found methods of mass producing steel in long continuous joists and bars... and REINFORCED CONCRETE was developed.

The concrete (cement, gravel, sand and water) took care of the compression, and embedded steel bars took care of the TENSION.

Reinforced concrete beams of relatively thin depth could span over vast distances... ideal for bridges, lighthouses, aircraft hangers. Concrete was cheaper and more fireproof than steel: floors, beams and walls could be formed at the same time.

This continuity of structure is the material's great advantage. It can be poured into any shape, with flowing plastic curves like this early pioneer 1913 Centenary Hall in Breslau by Max Berg...

or into long CANTILEVERS (beams or floors projecting with no end support)

or into posts and beams (like timber frames, only stronger and more durable) for cellular buildings... flats, offices, hotels. Auguste Perret, (1874–1954) pioneered the method in France.

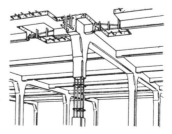

The second main feature of the modern Functional style is the glass wall. Steel and concrete frames liberated the outside walls of buildings from the task of supporting the roof and floors. Due to improvements in manufacturing plate glass, the outside walls could now be entirely translucent, giving the impression of infinite space...and bringing new problems in equal measure.

The third feature was the flat roof. The geometry of the traditional sloping roof or dome limited the plans of buildings to simple rectangles or a combination of rectangles. The flat roof enables the plans to be *any* shape. What was lost was storage space, space to hide water tanks and in rainy climates, the ability to throw the water off.

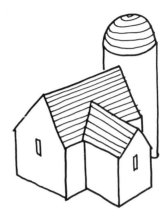

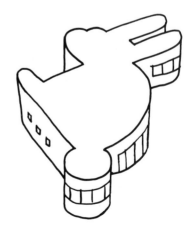

In Germany the shaky Weimar Democratic Republic built housing for the organised work force in the new style — white, pure, healthy. Rejecting the garden city layouts of houses and streets, the developments were in regimented blocks of flats with space between to let in light, sun and air.

An innovation was the provision of fitted kitchens but the flats were limited to the bare essentials to bring costs down to the level workers could afford.

STILL NO JOBS FOR ROOF TILERS

Many blocks were prefabricated. Whole walls were manufactured in factories and assembled on site to minimise production costs. This mechanisation, together with the use of the flat roof, put thousands of building workers, particularly roof-tilers, out of work and contributed to the growing unemployment...

114

THE BAUHAUS

The Modern Movement's search for principles and standards based on physical science and technology naturally found expression in architectural education. Until the First World War, training was by apprenticeship in an architect's office, or study in an academic institution where the rules of Classical composition were instilled. In 1919 Gropius set up the Bauhaus school in Weimar. Here the idea of **Basic Design** was developed which stemmed from a desire to apply scientific method to art. It was thought an artistic product could be broken down into (and hence built up from) its constituent parts like molecules — the basic elements of design. Not surprisingly, these turned out to be our old friends the cube, the sphere and the cone (or square, circle and triangle), all entirely colourless (white).

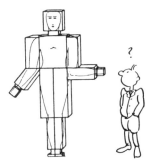

In 1924, faced with a right-wing administration in Weimar, the Bauhaus moved to Dessau. The recession was ending and the German economy was about to experience the economic boom of the 1920s. As before, it was based on heavy industry and machine production, especially armaments.

Gropius designed a new building for the school. It was a sensation and set the style of Modern Architecture from then on — the International Style.

The plan of the building was a free abstract composition which purported merely to fulfil the programme, free of formal preconceptions. The building, in other words, "designed itself". It contained all the ingredients of the "functional" style... steel-framing, large areas of glass, flat white cement bands, flat roofs... designed according to an abstract system of proportions. It was conceived as seen from above (the kamikaze pilot's view) or from a speeding car rather than at human eye level.

Both ended with the coming to power of the Nazis and the school was closed in 1932. Gropius, Mies and other Bauhaus luminaries fled to the US.

In fact the Nazis exploited any style that served their purpose at the time… first modern architecture, which was seen to be new and German, then Bavarian vernacular for the Hitler Youth and later German Romanesque for public buildings.

The new order, the new world, the new man… no longer an architectural dream, now a political reality. The Nazi style of building is nowadays seen to be the stripped and alien classicism of the firm of Hitler and Speer, the style of totalitarianism.

The Nazis' motto was "action without thought"… the antithesis of the modern architects'… strange then, that they should both arrive at the same point architecturally, destruction of the old, irrational, cluttered, human environment and its replacement by order and discipline…

119

THE US

The Industrial Revolution hit the US around 1860 on a vast scale, unencumbered by social and industrial traditions. Inside 20 years the US changed from having a rural economy based on small scale farming to an urban, industrial one. The railways, and coal, iron and steel production, coupled with unfettered private enterprise, transformed the country. By the end of the century, the machine, mass production and big business had made America the richest country in the world.

But wealth and power lay in the hands of a small group of multi-millionaires and groups of price-fixing companies in trusts. Capitalists like Rockefeller and Vanderbilt controlled governments by their power and wealth. They were like kings, and the mansions they had built were appropriately in French Absolute Monarch's Baroque.

Industrial America was built on cheap mass production — of tools, weapons, clothing, furniture and food. In contrast to Europe, materials were plentiful and skilled labour scarce. Mass produced goods were thus accepted, and mass production, not just using the new materials like cement and steel, but also brick, stone and especially timber, was the norm.

Factory-produced timber and cheap nails and screws gave rise to "balloon frame" structures (so called because of their lightness). Standard wooden sections were simply nailed together and stiffened by external match boarding, doing away with the traditional complex carpenter's joints. Here also, the machine made up for the lack of craftsmen. Houses built in this way were light, easy to prefabricate and transport... ideal for an expanding mobile population.

But while the Industrial Revolution made cheap houses available it transformed the buildings of industry and big business. As cities grew at a fast rate, downtown land increased in cost and the vast administrative centres required to run the enterprises started to expand upwards… into "skyscraper" office blocks.

But without the inventions of the Industrial Revolution skyscrapers would not have been possible…

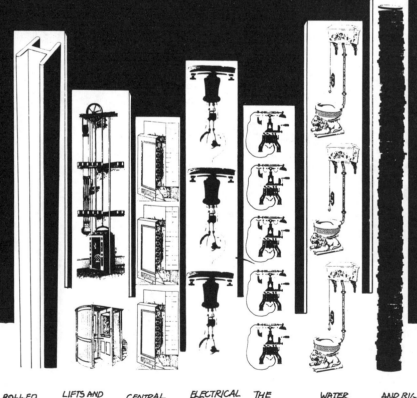

ROLLED
STEEL
JOISTS…

LIFTS AND
REVOLVING
DOORS…

CENTRAL
HEATING…

ELECTRICAL
LIGHT…

THE
TELEPHONE

WATER
CLOSETS
AND
PLUMBING

AND BIG
PROFITS

The needs of big business and the newly available technology enabled architects to design skyscrapers. But what should the *outsides* look like? There was no precedent for a 20 storey office block…

In New York the skeleton frames were clad in adapted versions of the historical styles… a gigantic classical column complete with base and capital… a Gothic church stretched out like toffee… several Renaissance palaces on top of each other… a gigantic Baroque castle…

But in Chicago, capital of the mid-west and less under European cultural domination, a manner of external styling determined by the grid of the structure was developed in the 1890s. This was seen as "honest" by the modern movement architects who took up the aesthetic.

As in England, industrial buildings on the waterfront had used cast iron framing on the outside together with large windows and classical ornament. Architects like the former military engineer Major William Le Barry Jenny (1832–1907), applied this to multi-storey structures of offices, hotels and high class apartment blocks... The grid appearance with long windows between the uprights became known as the **Chicago Style**.

The boldest examples of the Chicago style came out of the office of Adler and Sullivan. It was the perfect partnership. Adler was an engineer entrepreneur who contributed many structural innovations. Louis Sullivan was the artist philosopher who, although designing buildings for the new capitalists, had vague notions about a "democratic" architecture for, of and by "the people" related to truth to materials and structure. Sullivan's best known aphorism was "form follows function" by which he meant not that function equals beauty as the modernists later interpreted, but that utility and beauty should merge.

ART DECO

RUINED!

During the 1920s and 30s and through the Depression the move to the cities increased. The middle class settled in the suburbs and the mass-produced motor car, pioneered by Henry Ford, started to take over as the main form of transport. Capital put some of its vast profits into public "good works". In New York the Rockefeller Centre and Empire State buildings were built to staggering heights and both had public elements, one of which was Radio City. The 1930s ushered in the age of the entertainment industry, radio, movies, records, and for a while a new style flourished: Art Deco, the Jazz Age Baroque, a new dress for skyscrapers such as the Flat Iron and Chrysler buildings…

The origins of Art Deco are diverse. Its *eclectic* decorative style is a mixture of Red Indian symbolism, Cubism, Futurism, Expressionism and Egyptian, often applied to buildings in the form of coloured terracotta or glazed ceramic tiling.

In the 1940s and 50s the vast Movie Palaces in Europe and the US exploited Art Deco to the full, but generally the Second World War, and the Functionalists, put paid to it…

As we have seen, there are two basic approaches or modes in architecture... the **Classical** and the **Romantic**...

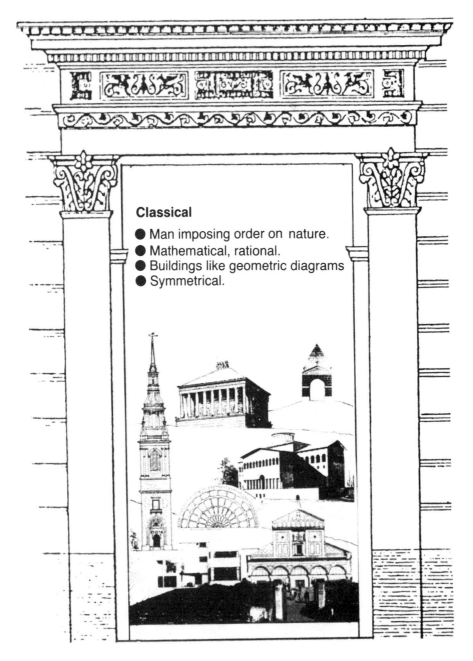

Classical

- Man imposing order on nature.
- Mathematical, rational.
- Buildings like geometric diagrams
- Symmetrical.

But there is no *pure* Classicism or Romanticism... the one always contains aspects of the other... the classical orders relate to natural form... the Gothic cathedral has a mathematical, harmonious discipline...

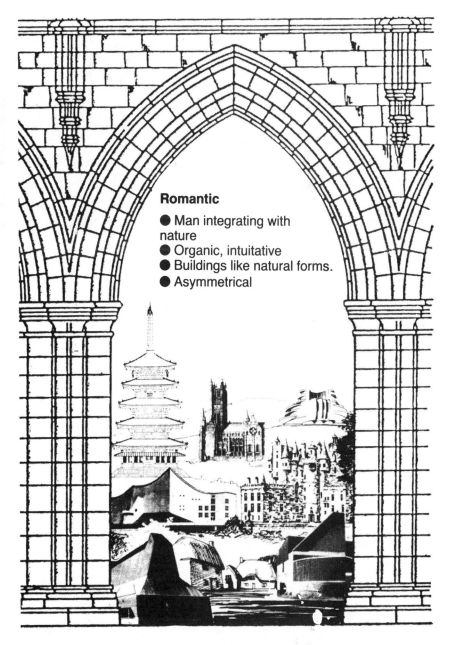

Romantic

● Man integrating with nature
● Organic, intuitive
● Buildings like natural forms.
● Asymmetrical

Modern architecture developed both the Romantic mode (Arts and Crafts, Art Nouveau, Expressionism) and the Classical (19th Century Engineering, Bauhaus, Functionalism).

But after the Second World War the rational, mechanistic, abstract classical side virtually devoured the other... the cube ate the flower. The Modern Movement became identified with the rectangular "functional" box... appropriate to a science-based industrial society...

These two early modern buildings in Holland demonstrate the contrasting approaches evolving from the same source...

ELEVATION

These two fundamental and contrasting, yet interdependent, ideals are personified in the work of the two great pioneering masters of modern architecture — Frank Lloyd Wright and Le Corbusier...

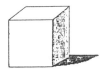

FRANK LLOYD WRIGHT

The works of Frank Lloyd Wright, America's best-known architect, spanned from the 1880s to the 1950s and represented a continuous link between the Modern Movement and its 19th Century origins.

Wright wanted to create an essentially American modern architecture — firmly rooted in vernacular indigenous forms. He was influenced by the English Arts and Crafts movement, Mayan and Amerindian native buildings, wooden structures of the American pioneers, and especially Japanese culture with its direct relationship to nature.

Wright's mystical romanticism stemmed from the great American 19th Century writers like Thoreau, Emerson, Melville, and the poet Walt Whitman. At the end of the century the wide open spaces of rural America still embodied the radical pioneering spirit, freedom of the individual and equality of opportunity in the Home of the Brave. Wright was a son of the mid-west, born a country boy, his father a Baptist preacher. After studying engineering for a while he set off for Chicago and fame. In 1887 he joined the office of Sullivan and Adler.

LE CORBUSIER

From the 1930s onwards the most influential architect of the Modern Movement was Le Corbusier. To most architects Le Corbusier was (and is) high priest, prophet and god in one. They hung on his every proclamation, received his latest projects with adulation and made endless pilgrimages to his few realised buildings. Le Corbusier *was* the Modern Movement.

Born Charles Edouard Jeanneret, son of a Calvinist Swiss watchmaker, he soon quit the family business to travel... to Paris to work for Perret, and to Germany as assistant to Behrens.

In 1913 Le Corbusier settled in Paris, then the centre of avant garde art, Cubism and Surrealism, where he invented *Purism.* Purism related the idea of the pure typical form, evolved through continual refinement (classicism), with the mass-produced artifacts of industrial society, which were basic forms refined by the economics of machine production. Modern Architecture was thus given respectability and a pedigree. It was not a "sham" copy of Classical architecture, but shared the same universal principles of reason, order and sophistication.

IT'S LE CORBUSIER!

NO, IT'S GOD, HE JUST THINKS HE'S LE CORBUSIER!

Wright developed the idea of **Organic Architecture** or building both at one with, and inspired by, natural forms.

He related great architecture to organic plant and animal forms and saw in the relationship of the parts to the whole, eternal laws and a connection between form and function. Following Sullivan he sought truth in nature's fundamental *principles* as opposed to surface *appearances.* The principles of Organic Architecture were developed in the Prairie House style. Its main elements were:

Horizontality.
Like Voysey, Wright saw the horizontal line as symbolising and evoking *oneness* with nature, as opposed to the vertical, which symbolises man's *domination* of nature.

Sympathy with the site.
Buildings should be designed to blend with the natural elements of the site. From Japanese temples Wright learned the art of merging building and landscape, blurring the division between inside and out.

Domestic symbolism.
Houses retain the traditional elements that evoke home, welcome, warmth, protection; pitched roofs, low ceilings and generous fireplaces at the centre, the heart from which other spaces radiate.

Truth to materials.
"Natural" materials such as brick, stone, wood and tile should be used untreated and not forced into shapes against their inherent nature.

Character.
Each house would be designed according to fundamental organic principles and the nature of the site as opposed to the application of one style. There should be as many styles as there are people.

Le Corbusier was by contrast a great exponent of the "scientific" method of "thinking out each problem afresh". For instance he took the traditional house and analysed it in the light of "cold reason":

Houses normally sat on the ground, "wasting" land. Using modern methods of construction the house could be raised off the ground on legs.

Houses had pitched (sloping) roofs which "wasted" space. With modern materials flat roofs could be built which provided extra space on top and underneath.

Houses had small, vertical windows. Modern construction enabled them to be in continuous bands wrapped round corners.

Gardens were usually on the ground at the back. They could be put on the roof thus saving more space.

Stairs wasted valuable internal space. Concrete ramps placed outside were more logical.

Walls previously had to be solid to support roof and floors. Concrete frames freed the walls from their structural function... they could be any shape or pattern.

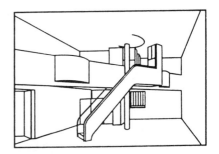

The inside used to be divided up into rooms with doors. Modern central heating enabled each floor to be one space... open planning.

Wright's Prairie Houses built up to 1910 were not located in wide open spaces but in the suburbs of Chicago. They were to house not free ranging pioneers, but affluent mid-west businessmen who had profited from the industrial expansion of the city and whose tastes were uncontaminated by the Europeanised eastern coast.

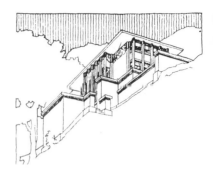

The Robie House of 1909 is the best known example. Wright exploded the tight European Arts and Crafts box into a free arrangement of dynamic, linear, expanding spaces. The low pitched cantilevered roofs hover protectively and reach out to encompass the surroundings.

Le Corbusier's best known pronouncement was "A house is a machine for living in", which has been interpreted to mean that a dwelling should be purely functional. Le Corbusier saw the house as a consumer product like a car to be wholly prefabricated in factories. With mass production houses would roll off the conveyor belts like Citroën automobiles, solving the housing problem at a stroke. This has been a particular obsession with architects ever since...

In fact Le Corbusier was inspired by *images* of machines and drew on these to create a new style unrelated to traditional architecture. His houses were intended to look like machines; each part was articulated like the components of a mechanical machine. Roof vent pipes were emphasised as on a liner. His best-known house, the Villa Savoye outside Paris, has been compared to a helicopter poised on a Virgilian landscape, related to the Classical and machine age ideals.

In 1911 Wright's work was published in Europe and had a huge influence.

But 1910-30 were the Wilderness Years, and Wright's work was rejected by the hard-line modernists for its romantic anti-collectivism and use of traditional materials and ornament. He was seen as the last of the 19th Century pioneers.

In fact Wright's use of modern technology was often far in advance of the Europeans'.

Among the many innovations he incorporated are the cantilever, central heating, air conditioning, double glazing, open planned kitchens, under floor heating and carports.

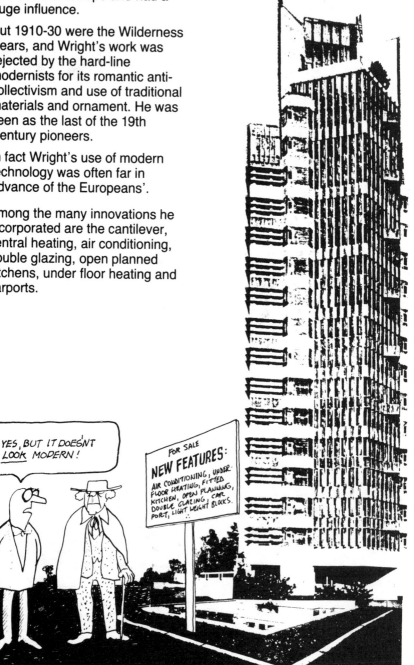

YES, BUT IT DOESN'T _LOOK_ MODERN!

FOR SALE
NEW FEATURES:
AIR CONDITIONING, UNDER
FLOOR HEATING, FITTED
KITCHEN, OPEN PLANNING,
DOUBLE GLAZING, CAR
PORT, LIGHT WEIGHT BLOCKS.

Le Corbusier's desire for *rationalism* (breaking down into constituent parts) ranged from town planning (zoning) through building functions, to elements of the building itself. He might *analyse* the window for example. The window's function is…
a) to let light in
b) to see out of
c) to let air in.

He might then design three *separate* elements for each function, to make an abstract pattern.

Whereas the traditional sash or casement window integrates these functions simply and economically, Le Corbusier taught architects to over-complicate in the name of innovation… to create more problems than were solved.

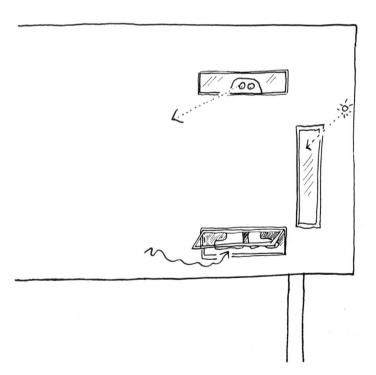

Wright was anti-city, anti-collectivism (which he called "mobocracy") and the money-centred urban society which the US was fast becoming. In the 1930s he developed his ideas for an ideal community called Broadacre City, a concept founded in the English Garden City idea, the American belief in a plentiful supply of land, and mystic notions of the human being's relationship with nature.

Broadacre City provided an acre of land for each family in a decentralised, low density, spaced out development run along agrarian economic principles of self sufficiency. The city included vinyards, baths, a circus, churches, craft workshops, stables, arboretums… everything for the pursuit of a civilised life. But the city did not exclude modern communication systems or provision for the car.

Broadacre City was never built and it was not until the 1970s that decentralised self-sufficiency came to be seen as a serious alternative to urban density.

WHY ARE ARCHITECTS LIKE STARLINGS?

BECAUSE THEY EAT IN THE COUNTRY AND CRAP IN THE CITIES !

Le Corbusier was a great exponent of the Futurists' idea of architecture as the expression of a new society. But rather than architecture determining the new utopia he saw the need to redesign society first and in his own image, as the cold intellectual, chaste and detached Nietzschean man.

His ideal society was to be ordered into neat packages where the individual was subservient to the centralised state.

Le Corbusier hated the "irrational mess" of cities like Paris and he drew up plans for rebuilding it along "rational" lines into neat rectangular plots or "zones". Each zone had a separate function… living, working, recreation, education… divided by motorways. At the centre, replacing the cathedral or town hall, were serried ranks of office towers housing the business industrialist controllers of society, the captains of industry. It was the most influential town planning idea of the 20th Century…

SACRE BLEU, I THINK I PREFER PARIS ZE WAY EET ESS!

In the 1930s Wright's practice expanded again with commissions for dwellings in rural settings. The most famous of these is "Falling Water" designed for the department-store tycoon Edgar Kaufmann on a rocky wooded site in Pennsylvania. Here architecture and nature merge. The rock forms part of the house which is built over a waterfall, in a series of daring reinforced concrete cantilevers.

Le Corbusier's dream of mass produced houses remained a dream. Unlike Germany, French building design was in the hands of the academies and the classicists. He had to be content with designing homes for rich art patrons in the suburbs of Paris, not machine made, but constructed in the traditional French method of rough block walls rendered over smooth and painted white, but without the vital copings, sills and overhangs.

In his 30's Swiss student's hostel in Paris, Le Corbusier developed his house-on-legs idea into a block for communal use.

CLEAN TIDY, FUNCTIONAL

A HOME FROM HOME!

Naturally these Cubist/Purist constructions soon deteriorated. Walls cracked and stained, windows rusted and the flat roofs leaked.

Being one step ahead of the other Modernists Le Corbusier altered his style accordingly...

The Johnson Wax office and research laboratories built at Racine between 1936 and 1948 typify Wright's approach… inspiration from organic structures, use of new technology and continuity through the innovatory use of traditional materials. Here the column supports are based on a mushroom or lilypad to produce a structural form in advance of its time.

The research tower is based on the tree: its basement the roots, its service core the trunk and its cantilevered floors the branches and foliage.

But externally the buildings are real Art Deco streamlined American architecture like a juke box, Cadillac or electric guitar.

Wright also designed high blocks of apartments, but not like the European "match-boxes". The Price Tower, Oklahoma, is firmly based on organic principles with Amerindian influences.

After the war, Le Corbusier abandoned the attempt to produce smooth machine-like surfaces and invented a new style he called "brutism" (from the French word meaning rough or raw). Concrete from crude timber shuttering was left purposely rough and untreated and was meant to have the qualities of an ancient ruin, battered and primeval...

Le Corbusier now advocated housing in the form of giant slabs or "Unités", set in their own parkland and containing all services like a small town.

The Socialist local authority in Marseilles commissioned a series of Unités from Le Corbusier, one of which was built. It was a "brut" concrete magnified version of the 1930s house, raised up on giant legs *(piloti)* articulated in its parts with blank ends and a roof to be used for communal recreation. Narrow maisonettes ran from front to back served by "internal streets". Architects hailed it as a masterpiece... it was housing turned into monumental sculpture, a floating monastery or a scaly prehistoric beast...! In reality the Unité was expensive, uncomfortable and out of tune with the needs of the working class families it was meant for. As the *buildings* obviously did not fit *people*, Corbusier redesigned *people* to fit the *buildings*... in the image of six-foot high Mr. Average Modular Man.

WRIGHT IN THE CITY...

After the Second World War Wright's work continued to flourish. His organic forms became freer and more plastic. He now drew on light but strong natural structures for inspiration — shells, cobwebs, or crystalline formations, such as the honeycomb.

When Wright built in the city he often abandoned the horizontal for the vertical, shutting out the surroundings behind solid-walled and top-lit spaces.

The design for his best known building of this period, the Guggenheim Museum in New York, is in the form of a huge ramped inverted spiral, once again top-lit, in reinforced concrete. Visitors are taken up to the top by lift and descend the ramp past paintings hung on the walls.

Wright even claimed that the structure had been designed to bounce like a spring in case of nuclear attack.

When Le Corbusier was not trying to be a social engineer he built some of the most successful, inventive and inspiring buildings of the Modern Movement. This was especially true when he designed for the Church, for spiritual absolutes rather than day-to-day needs. His monastery of La Tourrette or the chapel at Ronchamp, drawing on Greek village churches, comes closer than any other modern ecclesiastical architecture in evoking timeless spiritual qualities through new forms. They typify the best of Le Corbusier's work — powerful, assertive, innovatory, plastic, individual, puritan... and made by hand.

After the Second World War the Modern Movement, now dominated by the hard-line followers of Gropius, Mies and Le Corbusier, came into its own.

Its doctrine of large-scale building employing prefabricated industrial components and total reliance on advanced technology had anticipated the need for rapid rebuilding, together with the advances in machine production made during the war. Major resources were also available in a post war period of extensive industrialism and economic growth.

Modern architects assumed the role of missionaries... spreading the gospel to those with power or money or both... buildings designed according to the doctrines of modernism would be the salvation of the whole world... local cultures, traditions and social networks were irrelevant and outdated, and to deny this was heresy.

There would be, as Le Corbusier said, "one single building for all nations and climates".

HEALTH AND EFFICIENCY

Politicians were won over to the new architecture… in Europe new housing was desperately needed and the Modern Movement, following Gropius and Le Corbusier, had the answer… large-scale blocks of apartments, scientifically designed for light, air and health would rise up to replace the slums and bomb sites. Building high would be economic in land use *and* construction costs.

TO ACHIEVE A PLANNED ECONOMIC USE OF LAND AND RESOURCES . . .

THE PEOPLE MUST ABANDON THEIR TRADITIONAL HABITATS…

AND WE MUST EDUCATE THEM IN NEW WAYS OF…

LIVING !

Traditional methods of building in brick or timber were far too slow and limited for the task in hand. Prefabricated parts made in factories and rapidly hoisted into position by tower cranes was the 20th Century answer. Whole walls, whole rooms, whole houses could be mass-produced by machines... they were bound to be more efficient and longer-lasting than traditional materials. At least that was the hypothesis... now to test it experimentally on a vast scale...

PUBLIC AND PRIVATE

As in the past, like the pyramids or Baroque palaces, the new massive monumental structures symbolised and expressed the power of the ruling élite… in totalitarian countries it was the state monopolist bureaucracy… the ministries and administrative centres…

… and in the West the modern movement provided brand images for the giant business empires of consumer capitalism… prefabricated standardised office headquarters…

The facts of private wealth and ownership are usually concealed and elusive, but a building blatantly exposes them for all to see…

The post war world now comprised the two nuclear superpowers, the US and its Western dependent states, and the USSR and its satellites, with a poverty stricken "third world" still exploited for its cheap goods and labour — headed by China.

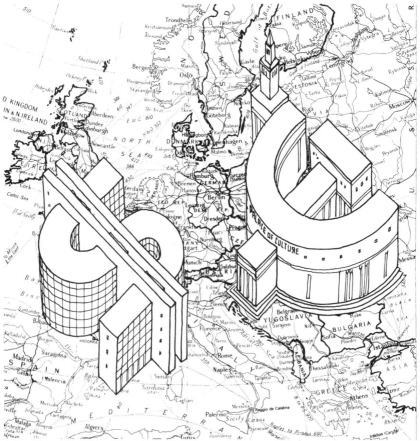

The new building for the United Nations, formed so that nations could talk rather than fight, was built in New York in the modern style. Unfortunately, the council debating chamber, which should be the key element, is dominated by a massive administrative tower… symbolic of the bureaucratic nature of political power… a modern Tower of Babel. As ever, architecture reveals the truth behind the intention…

In the mixed economies of Europe, both private capital and state bureaucracy erected their monuments, but in many areas the new architecture *did* serve progressive social aspirations.

..AFTER

The new Welfare States set up to protect and care for their citizens from the cradle to the grave found expression in the bright new buildings for schools, hospitals, clinics, universities or transportation. A new style for a better fed, better educated, expanding population...

HOSPITAL

Equally in the private sector, buildings for entertainment, shopping, sport, or work exploited the possibilities of modern architecture… For *new* building types, supermarkets or airports, the new style was often successful and popular.

But for older categories of architecture, housing and civic design particularly, the large-scale approach typified by the Modern Movement has become a world wide failure, both technically, culturally, climatically and socially…

TECHNICAL FAILURE

The Modern Movement believed that the exploitation of advanced technology would make buildings not only quicker to erect and cheaper, but of a higher standard. Thirty years on society is presented with a massive bill for putting right building failures either by repair, renovation or demolition. Why?

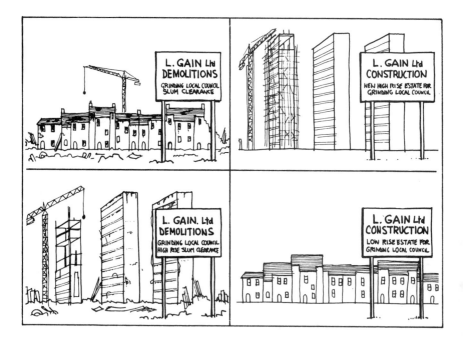

● Governments wanted to build quickly but with minimum cost. Standards were cut, bad enough in small buildings, but disastrous in large high structures.
● New techniques and materials (like many new drugs) were inadequately tested and understood. Many were positively dangerous to health… asbestos, cavity foam insulation, acrylic, high alumina cement, air conditioning, wood preservatives etc.

- Buildings are not machines… they cannot be discarded like obsolete cars or refrigerators... they have to last, the resources needed to build them are too great.
- The Modern Movement rejected ornament as irrelevant, but ornament was not just decorative. It helped to cover joints between materials and enabled buildings to "weather" by throwing off rain water from façades. To try to obtain a smooth jointless, machine-like appearance is costly and illogical. A truly rational approach would have studied traditional buildings to monitor the scientific reasons for their successes *and* failures.

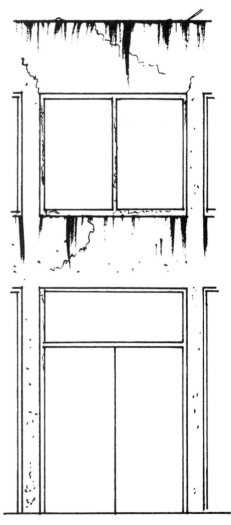

CLIMATE FAILURE

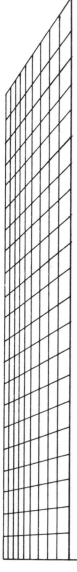

Even before the energy crisis of 1973, the failure of modern buildings to cope with a variety of climates was apparent.

They relied on technology to provide comfortable conditions internally — artificial ventilation, air-conditioning, central heating. Again local, traditional methods which had evolved simple and successful means of achieving comfort were ignored… Large areas of glass were employed in all climates, hot or cold. Orientation could be ignored, glass walls could face north in cold regions or south in hot. Just pump in/out more heat/air/moisture!

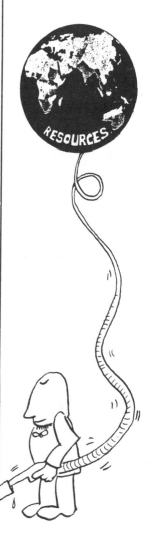

Unfortunately even in the few cases where sophisticated air-conditioning was affordable, the energy consumption required to compensate for thin construction was enormous. Most new buildings had to rely on cheap means of heating and ventilation and consequently acted like greenhouses, swelteringly hot in summer, freezing in winter, prone to massive condensation and harmful to health.

Modern architecture also ignores the micro climates traditionally created by low groups of buildings — shade, protection, shelter, warmth. High blocks create wind turbulence at ground level and cast huge shadows. Low blocks are often laid out as separate elements in a composition on paper (the legacy of abstract cubism) without thought for the windy or exposed spaces created between.

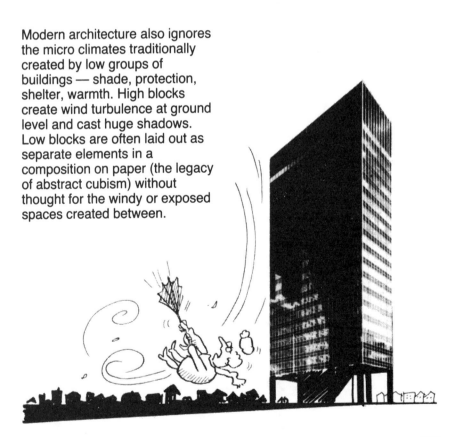

CULTURAL FAILURE

The Modern Movement was obsessed with the "machine aesthetic"; buildings had to *look* like machines to be "functional", and it was also influenced by narrow abstract cubist aesthetic principles. This ignored the potency of traditional symbols and the power of the ancient architectural language. Modern design attempted to impose its esoteric values and preconceptions on people who had different aspirations. It also became the tool of power groups who sought to eradicate old cultures which they saw as obstacles to their control.

All over the world traditional communities were broken up and forced into high rise apartment blocks, to be alienated and isolated, their old interdependence and self-help destroyed. Families with children were put into minimum accommodation with nowhere to play, dependent on cheap lifts which constantly broke down and with no contact with neighbours. The blocks belonged not to the people but to the state. The vast areas of territory no-one was responsible for — lifts, stairs, corridors, were consequently vandalised and graffitied.

SOCIAL FAILURE

In spite of the Modern Movement's aim to build an egalitarian utopia, architecture still serves élites and reinforces their power. In this sense it is, as always, a successful reflection of political and social realities.

Some architects blame Society, maintaining it gets the architecture it "deserves" as though somehow architects have no influence over what they do. Most people have no say, no power and no choice where their environment is concerned.

Modern architects have tried to be social engineers, determining *new social* structures by designing *new physical* forms, but this has been a hopeless failure. People will not be fitted into tidy patterns — thankfully, they resist it.

HIRED GUNS

After 50 years the large-scale solutions of the Modern Movement have not been accepted... people have resisted being re-educated to new ways of living... there is a deep conflict between architects' and planners' objectives, and the people they are supposed to serve.

Their "professional objectivity" looks more like patronising indifference, as socially unconcerned as that of traffic engineers...

… or hired guns for land speculators, abetting them in the destruction of well-loved old towns and city centres, and their replacement by profitable "concrete jungles".

PATRONAGE

Yet these same loved old towns and cities were built by private enterprise or authoritarian power... Why then does this not work today?

It is partly the scale of the development, more buildings have been built in the last 30 years than in the last 300, so more *bad* examples exist, and partly that craftsmanship and pride in work were driven out by the Modern Movement. But fundamentally, it is a question of patronage — the aims and motives of those who commission buildings.

In the past the patron of architecture was an emperor, pope, prince, king, capitalist... who desired a monument, but a monument of quality. They were invariably educated in matters of taste, talked the language of design, were able to make demands, choose the best architects... Ordinary houses were built by local builders, or the inhabitants, using tried and tested traditional methods.

The Modern Movement set out to serve the needs of *all* society... but this new role was tackled with the old methods... building monuments for élites in the name of the people...

In the public domain architects attempt to be doctors solving society's ills, but with insufficient resources. They are answerable to a bureaucracy and political masters often concerned with quantity rather than quality. The people the buildings are for have no say in what is provided.

In the private sphere architects are hired servants to big business and land speculators with large resources, who are answerable to management committees, accountants or boards of directors concerned with profit not quality, and who may never even see the building. The building users and local communities have no say.

PLUG IN, TURN ON, DROP OUT

The 1960s saw unprecedented Western affluence on the one hand and a prophetic cultural reaction to industrial society on the other.

Technology had put men on the moon, the ultimate waste of resources, and now anything was possible. Futurist architectural fantasies were the result, based on the indiscriminate employment of more and more advanced technology presented through clever pop sci-fi graphics... plug-in capsule cities... walking cities... living pods.

It was the Modern Movement's last fling... not the beginning of a new era but the end of the advanced industrial society.

I'M AFRAID YOU'VE JUST MISSED BIRMINGHAM – BUT GLASGOW WILL BE ALONG IN AN HOUR

At the same time the idea of the **alternative society** emerged, romantic, individualist, anti-capitalist, anti-state socialist... akin to the mid-19th Century movements. There was concern about the ecological and social destruction wrought by industrialism, and a desire for people and nature to coexist once more. For a time the abundance of alternative ideas in every field shook the political establishment, but by the 1970s these had dissipated or were absorbed by the pop music and fashion industry. The dream went sour, the State took an even firmer grip.

Alternative architecture was contained in the idea of self-sufficiency... the Eco House which recycled its waste, relied on low technology for its materials and was serviced by sun or wind power.

THE ERGONOMES

In the 1960s some architects believed that if the application of science to design had failed to produce an architecture fit for people it was because it was the wrong *sort* of science... physical science. If the relatively new *human* sciences (sociology, environmental psychology, anthropometrics, ergonomics etc.) could be harnessed, the problems of designing for unknown users would be solved... just send out teams of sociologists to find out "what people wanted".

However useful the social sciences are in confirming simple truths (which the professions often lose sight of) they cannot rationalise the activities of human beings and draw up universal laws of behaviour... people are just not predictable.

So architects created a mythical modern tribe… the Ergonomes or Mr and Mrs Average Statistic, who followed consistent patterns and lived in something called "community". It was thought modern architecture could re-create "community"… if people like streets then streets could be piled up one on top of the other in new blocks and so on. It was another patronising attempt to force people into Modern Movement preconceptions.

Of course there is no such being as an Average Person… people are made up of diverse individuals. Modern architecture proclaimed that it was for Everyman but ended up designing for "Nowhere Man"… creating an environment that positively hindered or excluded whole groups of individuals… disabled people, mothers, old people, children, tall people, small people, people with particular cultural or religious backgrounds…

THE MIDDLE EAST

The international Functional style was used all over the world as the tool of governments and powerful groups to destroy traditional culture and impose Western-inspired industrialisation. In this respect modern architecture is the most successful movement in the history of architecture!

NOW THAT WE'RE RICH AND POWERFUL, WE WANT ALL THE BENEFITS OF WESTERN TECHNOLOGY !

WELL, WE CAN PROVIDE THE EXPERTISE GAINED DURING OUR WIDE EXPERIENCE OF TRANSFORMING UNIQUE TRADITIONAL ENVIRONMENTS ...

After 1967, the Middle Eastern regimes, often run on near feudal lines, imported Western architects to modernise their towns and cities. The architects flocked to the new sources of wealth and power. Integrity, ethics or quality hardly came into it.

ARCHITECTURE AS LANGUAGE

Recent critics of the Modern Movement claim that it ignored the language of architecture developed over centuries in an attempt to produce functional and economical buildings. These buildings were largely neither functional nor economic but merely invented *metaphors* for these concepts... they expressed or celebrated the *process* of construction by revealing the structure as a *symbol* of machine efficiency or giving a gridded, graph paper appearance as a symbol of scientific method.

And too often modern buildings became malapropisms or unconscious mixed metaphors… attempting to say one thing but communicating another. If architects wish to elicit particular responses they must be in control of their language and recognise the power of historic architecture's complex vocabulary of meanings and symbols.

Modern architecture is like Esperanto, an attempt to invent and impose a common "rational" language and succeeding only in being incomprehensible and alien to the majority of people.

181

The language of architecture is built up of signs and symbols... specific shapes, forms and textures have specific meanings...

METAPHOR

shelter
security
privacy
ownership
warmth

important
elite
powerful
exclusive
expensive

hard
cold
calculating
business like
impersonal

entrance
gateway
porch
direction
importance

SIMILE

CLICHÉ

church   factory   bank   house

MALAPROPISM

house ?
factory ?
offices ?

As the Renaissance masters knew, buildings also relate to the human body (ANTHROPOMORPHISM). We say they "lie", "rise up", have "fronts" and "backs" and "faces", "silhouettes", "profiles", windows "look out" etc. Historically buildings had tops (heads or hats) related to the sky, middles and bases (feet) related to the ground. Like people they had shape or personality seen from a distance and individual features (detail) close to. Modern buildings often dispense with all this, they look alike from a distance and have no details to relate to. This is why they are called "inhuman", "faceless", "alien"… though architects *intended* them to communicate the opposite.

FRONT

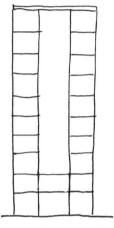

FRONT ? SIDE ?
BACK ?

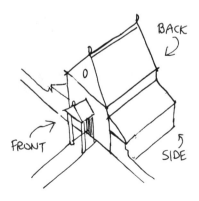

FRONT ?
BACK ?
ENTRANCE ?

SUBURBIA

As William Morris had looked beyond monumental architecture to humble people's own buildings, so the critics of the Modern Movement looked to contemporary housing which *did* appear to be successful and popular — the suburbs.

Modernists had condemned the suburbs for their wasteful sprawl, lack of planning and bourgeois life styles. Yet in England, eight million people had been rehoused in this way by speculative builders during 20 years of an inter-war economic depression.

Analysing the suburban house reveals a particular symbolism and imagery of home — security, individuality, privacy, contact with nature… a successful alternative to the Modern Movement's mass collectivist solutions.

In the US the suburbs, as in continental Europe, developed due to improved systems of transport communication to the city (railroad, streetcar, bus) and the increased prosperity of the lower middle classes. They tended to be more controlled and planned than in Britain, combining the ideals of the New England villa with Arts and Crafts principles. Frank Lloyd Wright had a big influence on the 1930s suburbs which were planned around the automobile.

POP ARCHITECTURE

American modern architects like Robert Venturi reacted against the monumental, abstract exclusiveness of the Modern Movement. Following Pop Art, he sought inspiration for a popular architecture in areas where commercial enterprise had created buildings and environments free from the constraints of architects or planners.

Las Vegas, the entertainment city in Nevada, for example, is a sprawling eclectic jumble of styles from modern to pseudo-Roman. Buildings are little more than sheds with signs and displays to attract customers off the road and into the gambling casinos.

At night a totally different environment is revealed, hidden by day, formed by the electric illuminations where space is defined, not by buildings, but by artificial light.

By analysing the apparent chaos of Las Vegas, Venturi attempted to evolve a self-conscious design philosophy for an "ordinary" and "inclusive" popular modern architecture of decorated sheds with obvious "fronts and backs" employing traditional signs and imagery.

He deliberately ignored the political and social aspects of Las Vegas, a gangster community which exploits greed and sexuality and pollutes its desert location.

POST MODERNISM

The outcome of all this questioning of Modern Movement principles is… confusion. Now anything goes. But we *can* chart four basic approaches (or styles) which have emerged: **Post Modern, Neo Vernacular, Neo Neo Classical and High Tech.**

Post Modernism aims to revert to the use of traditional language of sign and symbol while still using modern technology (similar to the way Mannerism elaborated Renaissance elements). It employs plastic decoration, aluminium column capitals, neon pediments and "trompe l'oeil", where one material pretends to be another (e.g. "marbelising" wood, colouring cement to look like stone).

POST MODERN!? BUT WHERE'S THE POST?

Oo.

Post Modernism rummages through history for reference — Egyptian, Classical, Art Deco, Bauhaus — and aims to make buildings work on two levels (Double Coding) so they can be appreciated by architects *and* "ordinary people".

The trouble is that it is dangerous to set out to be popular… sticking ornament on to standard office blocks and making sky-scrapers in the form of 18th Century clocks may be more fun but it does not necessarily make them acceptable to the public. It smacks of more élitist games *by* architects *for* architects.

NEO VERNACULAR

As we have seen, vernacular-based modern architecture never completely disappeared. In the 1950s it re-emerged in Scandinavia, England, and in the work of architects like Alvar Aalto (1898–1976) in Finland. It combined Expressionist form with "natural" materials and modern planning and technology to produce a kind of International Vernacular, often identifiable by its use of pitched roofs and brickwork on large scale buildings.

It aimed to be "contextual", that is, determined by the site context, fitting in with old buildings and respecting existing patterns or routes.

At worst New Vernacular is used to dress up traditional large-scale bureaucratic or commercial anonymity in fake folksy dress. At best it represents the acceptable, popular and successful face of modern architecture.

NEO NEO CLASSICISM

In one of the Greek myths the god Antaeus drew strength from the ground. However many times he was felled he always rose up with renewed vigour.

Could it be that classical architecture is like Antaeus? Seemingly killed off by the Modern Movement it is making a comeback... it is certainly popular, or is it?

The classical system could be applied equally to a humble house or a grand palace, but in Europe it has come to be associated with power and the ruling class. In its stripped down version it evokes fascist or totalitarian repression.

"Columns for the people" was the cry in the USSR in the 1930s. Ricardo Bofill today designs massive workers' housing blocks in the form of a Colosseum or Triumphal Arch, but in prefabricated concrete parts without the detail and scale of true classicism. It fulfils Le Corbusier's dream of uniting technology and classical architecture with a scale and power which makes the former's Unités look like dolls' houses.

HIGH TECH

The Modern Movement is still very much around, especially where big business is concerned.

High Tech or Late Modern is the new multinational style, claiming to have overcome the dreadful environmental defects of earlier steel and glass boxes by using up-to-date technology.

For British High Tech superstars like Norman Foster or Richard Rogers, heavy masonry construction went out with the steam engine. Drawing on aircraft technology, their exposed structures are light and strong, using heavily insulated wall panels, steel and aluminium frames and mirror glass in neoprene gaskets.

High Tech is unashamedly a style but its colours and forms celebrate the Modern Movement. Its forté is in light spacious sheds where all the services (like ventilation ducts, pipes or even stairs) are placed *outside* the building to leave free uninterrupted floor space where layouts for offices, exhibition halls, or factories can be changed at will (flexibility).

High Tech tends to be very expensive, wasteful of energy and lousy for housing.

MULTI-NATIONAL NEO-COLONIALISM

Whatever the style, architecture continues to serve power, wealth and corruption. Multi-national global economics mean capital operates internationally, while labour and politics are still static and national. Capital scours the Third World for the cheapest labour to exploit. The whole world is their colony.

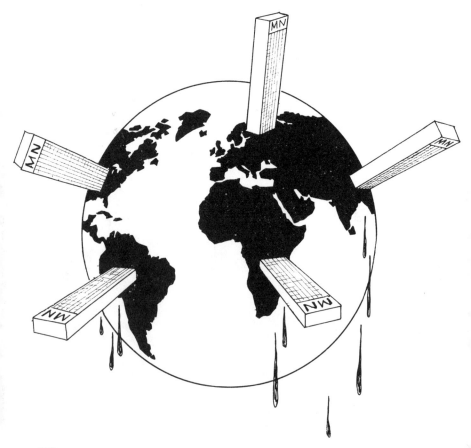

The architecture of multi-nationalism is typified by the Hong Kong and Shanghai bank by Norman Foster. The building components come from all over the world, from Germany to New Zealand. The site could be anywhere where labour is cheap and government docile.

MODERN JAPAN

Le Corbusier's dream of producing buildings like motor cars to be distributed all over the world remains a dream. Even the International Style is modified by local character. When Japan emerged as a world economic force it adopted Western modern architecture, not having any tradition of monumental large scale forms of its own. The early modern Japanese buildings by architects like Kenzo Tange often evoked traditional timber structures.

The traditional qualities of precision and organisation which are partly responsible for Japan monopolising the world electronics industry is *not* reflected in its modern architecture. The later buildings by architects like Arata Isozaki have shed all traditional influences in pursuit of multi-national ostentation. This is a reflection perhaps of modern Japan where a handful of industrial giants control every aspect of society from politics to leisure.

THE POST INDUSTRIAL SOCIETY

TECHNOLOGY
This variety or confusion mirrors perhaps the current painful Western transition to a post industrial society or crisis of capitalism, however you like to see it. Hopefully, the features of such a society, if it survives, will be self-reliance, low technology, a return to handicraft, more leisure and local political involvement.

Low technology will replace high. The massive post-war building boom based on economic growth is not likely to happen on such a scale. The task will be to repair decaying fabric of towns and cities and find new uses for old buildings.

Computers should improve performance by rapidly monitoring and calculating all those aspects of buildings that are quantifiable. The bad news for architects is that computers can also rapidly do perfect finished drawings from rough sketches...

CLIMATE

After the oil crisis of 1973 and the realisation that supplies of fossil fuels would eventually run out, governments looked to methods of reducing energy consumption. Buildings use over 50% of all energy, not including the manufacture of materials and construction. Renewable sources of energy from the sun, wind, water, earth... were also investigated.

Initially, there were numerous designs for *autonomous* houses which were self-sufficient and did not rely on external centralised sources of energy or food. The sun or wind was harnessed to heat water and run batteries; sewage and waste wre recycled as fertiliser; food was grown in conservatories and gardens. However, these houses became so gadget ridden that it was almost a full-time job to keep them running!

Now there is more emphasis on *passive* energy use — exploiting the form of the building, its siting and orientation for conservation — using trees and earth as barriers against the cold or wind or heat, building up heat in conservatories to be recycled in living areas, providing high insulation and thick walls that store heat. We are learning from the defects of previous modern environments, combined with the study of the values contained in old buildings.

MODERN BUILDINGS WITH THIN CONSTRUCTION ARE PRONE TO HEAT LOSS (A), CONDENSATION (B) AND EXPOSURE TO COLD (C)

PASSIVE USE OF ENERGY PROVIDES A BARRIER ROUND THE BUILDING ~ A GLASS CONSERVATORY ON THE SOUTH SIDE WITH HEAVY INSULATION ON THE NORTH AND UNDER SIDES.

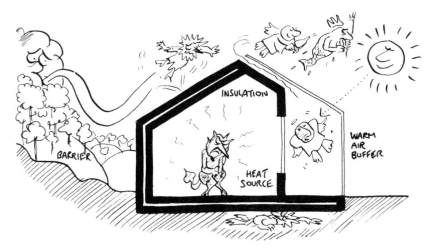

SOCIETY

The post industrial society, with no industrial base or growth economy may well move away from mass collective concentrations of people and away from state monuments to the "housing problem", or the "education problem" or the "old age" problem! Such bureaucratic solutions are isolated from the communities they serve. There may be a move to the countryside, to dispersal and community self-help. This will entail small-scale buildings, as adaptable as old terrace housing, either by renovating existing buildings (by DIY self-build or local builders) or the addition of new infill.

The massive political and economic forces that crush our lives and hopes will no doubt still exist and some architects will continue to serve them, designing their strongholds ever more fortified against "terrorism" and concealing nuclear bunkers for officials. But others will learn to relate directly to people, not replacing old abstract notions of "society" with new abstract concepts of "community", but working face to face with groups of individuals.

PUBLIC SECTOR

PRIVATE SECTOR

SELF BUILD.

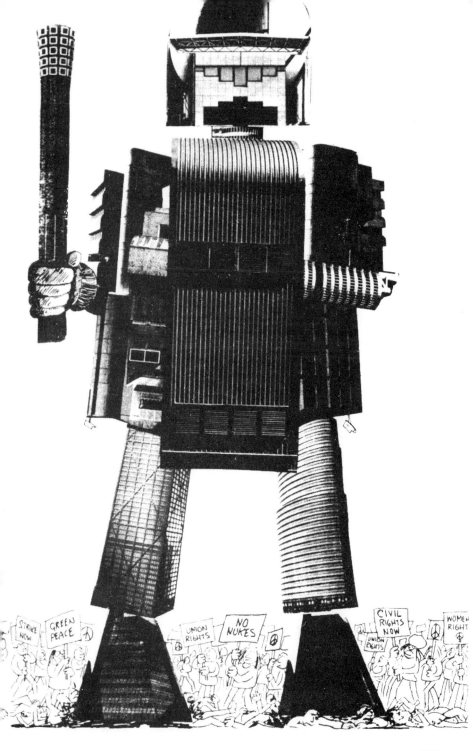

CULTURE

The present architectural debate about which style is most appropriate or popular is irrelevant. The key factor is, as ever, political — while people have cultural solutions imposed on them there will be problems — the only hope lies in people having direct control over their environments.

Architecture is about more than just appearance or choosing from the latest fashionable style.

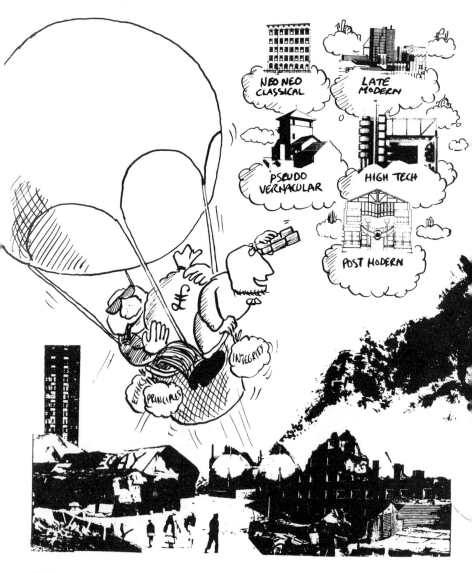

Those who look back to the architecture of the past usually do so in an attempt to recreate it and the kind of society that spawned it, rather than to learn from its lessons.

They, along with the media, diplay the same faults as the arrogant modernists they condemn in claiming to speak for 'ordinary people', whom they portray as rejecting *all* modern architecture as opposed to its worst excesses.

Functionalism failed because it was successful. All over the world it was hi-jacked by authority unconcerned with its initial ideals. Its desire to build on a massive scale and act as social engineering may have failed, but many of the basic ideals are still valid.

For William Morris the new architecture was to be democratic, serving all society, not just a privileged élite. This battle is still being fought.

Functionalism rejected the need for colour, texture, complexity and ornament. But these qualities exist, not just in the historic styles, but in 20th century architecture in its widest sense, a rich and varied source which we are just starting to tap...Art Deco, Art Nouveau, Expressionism etc...

The Modern Movement may have failed, but it failed heroically in an attempt to confront the facts of industrial society and come to terms with, for instance, mass production.
We have since recognised that the products of the machine do not need to be machine like themselves. These two buildings, for example, are both erected by hand from mass produced industrial components. Which is the more *modern?*

Current developments are not an *alternative* to modern architecture but its flowering. Modern architecture *is* the architecture of our industrial age, a third style to place alongside the Classical and the Gothic...

BUILDINGS ILLUSTRATED

Page

Page

BIBLIOGRAPHY

A History of Architecture on the Comparative Method Sir Banister Fletcher, Batsford 1896.
A formidable tome. The architect's Encyclopaedia Britannica. Constantly revised. Contains everything you need to know.

The Story of Art E.H.Gombrich, Phaidon 1950.
The beginning of each chapter makes a beautifully concise potted history of architecture.

An Outline of European Architecture N. Pevsner, Penguin 1943.
Varied in quality but a must all the same.

A Concise History of Western Architecture R.Furneaux Jorden, Thames and Hudson 1969.
Fairly straightforward view but well written.

The Observer Book of Architecture Penoyre and Ryan, Wane 1958.
The best of the 'pocket' books on the subject.

Pioneers of Modern Design N. Pevsner, Penguin 1936.
An unrepentant Modernist's view. Not to be missed!

Guide to Modern Architecture R.Banham, Architectural Press 1982.
By the guru of the Modern Movement.

The Language of Post Modern Architecture C.Jencks, Academy 1977.
Best selling trendy guide to the Baroque mode of modernism. Witty new journalese. All options open.

The Failure of Post Modern Architecture Brent C.Bolam, Studio Vista 1976.
Early exposé of crass Functionalism. The author is an architect for a change.

From Bauhaus to Our House Tom Wolfe, Cape 1982.
Summed up in the dreadful title pun. Written in total ignorance of architectural history but hilariously gets to the nub all the same.

The publisher gratefully acknowledges the following sources:

Academy Editions. C.Jencks. *Free Style Classicism.*
    for: Housing at Marne-la-Vallée, France 1984.
Architectural Design.
    for: Eco Houses; Plug-In City; Walking City 1964–66.
The Architectural Press. R.Banham. *Guide to Mordern Architecture.*
    for: CLASP School, England 1960.
The Architectural Press. *The Architect's Journal.*
    for: Broadleys, Windermere 1878; Mansion House Square tower. Mies van der Rohe;
    Red Cross HQ, Tokyo 1977; The Red House, London 1859.
The Architectural Press. *The Architectural Review* .
    for: Capital; Vernacular houses.
Barker. W. Taylor. *Greek Architecture.*
    for: Acropolis and Propylaea Mid 5th century BC.
Blue Circle. J.Prizeman. *Your House.*
    for: Suburban houses.
Built Environment.
    for: German Gothic illustration.
Dover N.Y. C.M.Harris. *An Illustrated Dictionary of Historic Architecture.*
    for: Caryatid from Erechtheion 421–405 BC; Izumo Shrine, Japan 5th century AD;
    Kondo at Horiuji, Japan 7th century AD.
Hamish Hamilton. S.Steinberg. *The Labyrinth* .
    for: Cartoon.
Hamlyn. Copplestone. *World Architecture.*
    for: Mesopotamian temple; Ziggurat at Ur 2125 BC.
Macmillan. J. Hawkes. *The Atlas of Early Man.*
    for: Han House. 500 BC; Skin and bone house, Siberia; Stick house, Yugoslavia.
MIT Press. R.Venturi etc. *Learning From Las Vegas.*
    for: Las Vegas, US.
Morgan-Grampian Ltd. *Building Design* .
    for: Vernacular houses.
Pelican. Frankfort. *The Pelican History of Architecture:*
                    Art and Architecture of the Ancient Orient.
    for: Ziggurat, Khorsabad 722–705 BC.
Pelican. N.Pevsner. *An Outline of European Architecture.*
    for: Church.
Scientific American.
    for: Structure of a Gothic Cathedral.

HOW TO GET GREAT THINKERS TO COME TO YOUR HOME...

To order any current titles of Writers and Readers *For Beginners*™ books, please fill out the coupon below and enclose a check made out to **Writers and Readers Publishing, Inc.** To order by phone (with Master Card or Visa), or to receive a <u>free catalog</u> of all our *For Beginners*™ books, please call (212) 982-3158.

Price per book: $11.00

Individual Order Form   (clip out or copy complete page)

Book Title	Quantity	Amount
	Sub Total:	
N.Y. residents add 8 1/4% sales tax		
Shipping & Handling ($3.00 for the first book; $.60 for each additional book)		
	TOTAL	

Name _____

Address _____

City _____ **State** _____ **Zip Code** _____

Phone number (___) _____

MC / VISA (circle one) Account # _____ **Expires** _____

Send check or money order to: **Writers and Readers Publishing**, P.O. Box 461 Village Station, New York, NY 10014 (212) 982-3158, fx (212) 777-4924; In the U.K: **Airlift Book Company**, 8, The Arena, Mollison Ave., Enfield, EN3 7NJ, England 0181.804.0044. Or contact us for a <u>FREE CATALOG</u> of all our *For Beginners*™ titles.

Writers and Readers